150 Vegan Favorites

150 Vegan Favorites

*Fresh, Easy, and
Incredibly Delicious
Recipes You Can
Enjoy Every Day*

Jay Solomon

PRIMA HEALTH

A Division of Prima Publishing

© 1998 by Jay Solomon

PRIMA HEALTH and colophon are trademarks of Prima Communications, Inc.

Library of Congress Cataloging-in-Publication Data

Solomon, Jay.
   150 vegan favorites / Jay Solomon.
     p.   cm.
   Includes index.
   ISBN 0-7615-1243-8
   1. Vegan cookery. I. Title.
TX837.S665 1998
641.5'636—dc21   98-4849
                                    CIP

     00 01 HH 10 9 8 7 6 5
Printed in the United States of America

How to Order
Single copies may be ordered from Prima Publishing, 3000 Lava Ridge Court, Roseville, CA 95661; telephone (800) 632-8676. Quantity discounts are also available. On your letterhead, include information concerning the intended use of the books and the number of books you wish to purchase.

Visit us online at www.primalifestyles.com

Contents

Introduction

Welcome to *150 Vegan Favorites,* a compilation of innovative and traditional vegan dishes culled from around the world. This grand world of vegan cuisine explores the adventurous possibilities of cooking with vegetables, grains, legumes, and fruits. From savory soups, crisp salads, and piquant dips to hearty one-pot dishes, pilafs, and pastas, here is gourmet vegan fare prepared with culinary flair.

In addition to pleasurable flavors and soothing aromas, plant-based vegan cookery offers a wealth of health benefits. In *150 Vegan Favorites,* there are myriad recipes loaded with nutritious foods such as dark leafy greens, winter squash, whole grains, beans, and seasonal fruits. These "power foods" provide antioxidants, phytochemicals, fiber, complex carbohydrates, and other vital nutrients that help prevent and fight chronic disease, bolster the immune system, provide energy, and enhance the overall quality of life. The vegan diet—a vegetarian regime that excludes all dairy and animal byproducts such as cheese, milk, and eggs—is also naturally low in fat and calories and cholesterol-free.

In the past the vegan diet has occasionally been labeled as too restrictive or austere. To the contrary, the new brand of vegan cookery is not limited to sprouts, nuts, and granola. Today's vegan pantry overflows with wild rice, couscous, arborio rice, red lentils, chick-peas, potatoes, yams, and pastas galore. Seasonal vegetables such as winter squash, woodsy mushrooms, colorful leafy vegetables, and tropical fruits are in great demand, as are fresh herbs, spicy chilies, glorious garlic, and fragrant spices. Of course, soy milk, rice milk, and tofu are stalwart (and versatile) staples. The culinary possibilities are endless.

The dishes in this book are sure to be a boon to the harried cook whose supper hour seems more like a rush hour. Many of the user-friendly recipes can be prepared in thirty minutes or less and are easy to follow. Most of the ingredients are readily available in well-stocked supermarkets and natural food stores—and won't send you scurrying on a treasure hunt (or break your budget). The wide selection of recipes inspires inviting menu ideas for every season and occasion.

Whether you are a vegetarian, vegan, or just striving to decrease the meat and dairy products in your diet, you will enjoy this bountiful collection of high-spirited and adventurous recipes. *150 Vegan Favorites* offers vivid proof that meatless, dairy-free meals can be appealing, nourishing, and immensely gratifying. So fire up the stove and rally your appetite; these vibrant vegan recipes promise to satisfy with epicurean delight.

Happy cooking!

Chapter 1

Savory Soups and Delicious Chilies

A steaming bowl of hot soup or wholesome chili beckons with warmth and goodness. Hearty soups and chilies nourish and replenish the appetite as well as the spirit. Whether as a prelude to dinner or as a light meal with warm bread, a well-filled bowl leaves a lasting and memorable impression. This is the ultimate comfort food.

Vegan soups and meatless chilies are a boon to the health-minded cook. The flavorings of yesteryear—such as heavy cream, butter, and ground meat—have been eclipsed by today's new culinary stars: garden herbs, garlic, chili peppers, and a smorgasbord of spices. Hardy staples such as winter squash, whole grains, beans, and root vegetables fill the bowl as well to quench the appetite.

Making a soup or chili is a most forgiving kitchen endeavor—almost anyone can create a simmering pot filled with vibrant flavors. If you can chop, stir, and slurp, then you have made the team. All you need is an assortment of fresh ingredients and pantry staples, a sturdy pot, and a little time to simmer and stir. The ability to follow a recipe helps, but it is not a prerequisite. Most recipes are intended to be general blueprints, not precise instructions.

Here are four basic steps that guide the recipes in this chapter.

Step One: Create an Aromatic Base with Sautéed Vegetables

A well-made soup or chili begins with sautéed vegetables—what Italians call *soffrito* and the French call *mirepoix*. To create this aromatic base, briefly cook a mixture of vegetables over high heat in a small amount of liquid (either oil or wine). Sautéing the vegetables first—as opposed to stewing them in the broth—seals in the flavors and subtly sweetens the pot.

One basic combination of vegetables includes chopped onion, celery, and garlic. Depending on the recipe, you can add mushrooms, zucchini, eggplant, bell peppers, carrots, and other vegetables. In Creole and Cajun kitchens, the trio of onion, bell pepper, and celery is known as the "holy trinity." For a hot and spicy nuance, try jalapeño or serrano chili peppers; for a smoky flavor, a chipotle pepper works. Asian-style soups rely on chopped fresh ginger root, lemongrass, and garlic. A variety of wild mushrooms will add woodsy, earthy flavors to the pot. The possibilities are endless.

Step Two: Add Body and Substance with Harvest Vegetables and Seasoned Broths

After the vegetables have been sautéed, it is time to add the cooking liquid, either stock, water, or canned tomatoes, along with the dried seasonings and the bulk of the ingredients, such as potatoes, winter squash, carrots, and/or root vegetables. The stock gives the simmering pot a personality; herbs and spices give it flavor and character; and hardy starches give it body and structure. When combined and simmered, these main ingredients are responsible for the look, taste, and texture of the meal.

Step Three: Simmer, Steep, and Stir

For this stage, patience is a virtue: the soup or chili should slowly simmer over medium-low heat. Soups and chilies benefit from long spells of slow cooking (and occasional stirring), but these recipes do not require a lot of fuss or attention. During this stage, a kind of culinary alchemy takes place: potatoes, squash, and vegetables become tender, liquids thicken, garlic and herbs spread their aromatic presence. Flavors are coaxed, awakened, and united; appetites are nurtured.

Step Four: Add Last-Minute Finishing Touches

Near the end of the cooking time is the perfect moment for a last-minute touch. In the past, this often meant swirling in gobs of cream, butter, or salt, but in today's healthy vegan kitchen there are more inventive and nutritious approaches. For instance, stirring in fresh parsley, basil, arugula, chives, or scallions is an easy way to perk up the pot. Fresh herbs lose their potency over a long cooking time but bring a refreshing taste when added near the finish. A twist of freshly ground black pepper or a sprinkling of chopped onion or scallions adds uplifting flavors as well.

Of course, the last step is the easiest: ladle the soup or chili into warm bowls and pass the spoons and napkins. Whole wheat bread, corn bread, or soup crackers are natural companions, and for a dash of spice, offer a bottle of hot sauce at the table. With the right ingredients and recipe, the bowl will surely be good to the last drop.

Like fine wines, soups and chilies improve with age. Most recipes can be prepared one or two days ahead of time and refrigerated for later enjoyment. The flavors intermingle and meld and actually improve with time. So don't shy away from preparing large batches—today's leftovers can be savored tomorrow.

Hearty Barley and Wild Rice Soup

This chunky soup is filled with wholesome flavors and soothing textures. Although wild rice and barley are long-cooking grains, the wait is well worth it.

Yield: 6 servings

1	tablespoon canola oil
12	ounces white mushrooms, sliced
1	red bell pepper, seeded and diced
1	medium yellow onion, diced
2	large cloves garlic, minced
6	cups water
¼	cup barley
¼	cup wild rice
¼	cup dry white wine
1	medium sweet potato, diced
2	teaspoons dried oregano
½	teaspoon dried thyme
½	teaspoon salt
½	teaspoon black pepper

In a large saucepan, heat the oil over medium heat. Add the mushrooms, bell pepper, onion, and garlic and cook, stirring, for 8 minutes. Add the water, barley, wild rice, and wine and bring to a simmer over medium-high heat. Reduce the heat to medium and cook for 10 minutes, stirring occasionally. Add the sweet potato, oregano, thyme, salt, and pepper and cook for 35 minutes over medium-low heat, stirring occasionally. Remove from the heat and let stand for 5 to 10 minutes before serving.

Ladle the soup into bowls and serve with warm bread.

Fabulous Vegetarian Chili

Textured vegetable protein gives this delicious chili a chewy texture and earthy flavor.

Yield: 6 servings

1	tablespoon canola oil
1	small yellow onion, diced
1	red bell pepper, seeded and diced
2	large cloves garlic, minced
1	large jalapeño or serrano chili pepper, seeded and minced
1	cup textured vegetable protein (TVP)
1	cup water
1	can (28 ounces) crushed tomatoes
1	can (15 ounces) red kidney beans, drained
1	can (14 ounces) stewed tomatoes
1½	tablespoons chili powder
2	teaspoons ground cumin
½	teaspoon ground cayenne
½	teaspoon salt

In a medium saucepan, heat the oil over medium heat. Add the onion, bell pepper, garlic, and chili pepper and cook, stirring, for 5 minutes. Add the textured vegetable protein and water and cook for 5 minutes over medium-low heat, stirring occasionally. Add the crushed tomatoes, beans, stewed tomatoes, chili powder, cumin, cayenne, and salt and bring to a simmer over medium-high heat. Reduce the heat to medium-low and cook for about 15 minutes, stirring occasionally.

Remove from the heat and ladle the chili into large bowls. Serve with warm corn bread.

Helpful Tip:

Look for textured vegetable protein (TVP) in the bulk food section of natural food stores and well-stocked supermarkets.

Mexican Minestrone

This recipe combines the flavors of Mexico and Italy into one intensely flavored soup.

Yield: 4 servings

1	tablespoon canola oil
2	large carrots, diced
1	medium yellow onion, diced
1	red or green bell pepper, seeded and diced
3	or 4 cloves garlic, minced
1	jalapeño chili pepper, seeded and minced
2	cans (14½ ounces) vegetable broth
2	tablespoons tomato paste
2	teaspoons dried oregano
1	teaspoon dried basil
1	teaspoon ground cumin
½	teaspoon black pepper
4	ounces spaghetti or linguini, snapped in half
1	cup cooked or canned red kidney beans, drained
1	can (11 ounces) corn kernels, drained

In a large saucepan, heat the oil over medium-high heat. Add the carrots, onion, bell pepper, garlic, and jalapeño and cook, stirring, for 7 minutes. Add the broth, tomato paste, oregano, basil, cumin, and pepper and bring to a simmer over medium-high heat, stirring occasionally. Stir in the pasta, beans, and corn and return to a simmer. Cook until the pasta is al dente, 10 to 12 minutes, stirring occasionally. Remove from the heat and let stand for 5 minutes before serving.

Ladle the soup into shallow bowls and serve at once.

Curried Squash with Winter Greens

Winter squash melds well into soups and bisques. For this mellifluous offering, butternut squash teams up with sturdy leafy greens and assertive curry spices.

Yield: 6 servings

1	tablespoon canola oil
1	large yellow onion, diced
2	stalks celery, diced
2	large tomatoes, diced
3	or 4 cloves garlic, minced
2	teaspoons minced fresh ginger root
1	tablespoon curry powder
2	teaspoons ground cumin
1	teaspoon ground coriander
1	teaspoon salt
½	teaspoon black pepper
4	cups peeled, diced butternut squash
5	cups water
2	to 3 cups coarsely chopped spinach, chard, or kale

In a large saucepan, heat the oil over medium heat. Add the onion and celery and cook, stirring, for 5 minutes. Add the tomatoes, garlic, and ginger and cook, stirring, for 3 to 4 minutes. Stir in the curry powder, cumin, coriander, salt, and pepper and cook for 1 minute over low heat. Add the squash and water and bring to a simmer over medium-high heat. Reduce the heat to medium-low and cook until the squash is tender, about 25 minutes, stirring occasionally. Stir in the greens and cook for 10 minutes.

Transfer to a food processor fitted with a steel blade (or to a blender) and process until smooth, about 10 seconds.

Ladle the soup into bowls and serve at once.

Caldo Verde

Caldo verde, which means "green soup" in Portuguese, is a delicious and unpretentious tureen of kale, potatoes, white beans, and parsley.

Yield: 6 servings

1	tablespoon olive oil
1	medium yellow onion, chopped
2	or 3 cloves garlic, minced
4	cups water
4	cups peeled, diced white potatoes
½	teaspoon salt
½	teaspoon black pepper
2	cups chopped kale or green chard
1	can (15 ounces) white kidney beans, drained
¼	cup diced roasted red bell peppers
¼	cup chopped fresh parsley

In a large saucepan, heat the oil over medium heat. Add the onion and garlic and cook, stirring, for about 4 minutes. Add the water, potatoes, salt, and pepper and bring to a simmer over medium-high heat. Reduce the heat to medium and cook for 20 to 25 minutes, stirring occasionally.

Stir in the kale, beans, roasted peppers, and parsley and cook for 10 to 15 minutes. Remove from the heat and let stand for about 10 minutes. To thicken, mash the potatoes against the side of the pan with the back of a large spoon.

Ladle the soup into bowls and serve with warm French bread.

Helpful Tip:

Roasted red bell peppers are available in jars in the relish/pickle section of grocery stores.

Beet Vichyssoise

This alluring combination of beets, leeks, and herbs is a feast for the palate as well as the eyes. Fresh dill adds a delightful herbal nuance.

Yield: 6 to 8 servings

1	tablespoon canola oil
1	medium yellow onion, diced
2	cups chopped leeks
2	cloves garlic, minced
6	cups water
3	cups peeled, diced beets (2 to 3 beets)
2	cups peeled, diced white potatoes
¼	cup dry red wine
1½	tablespoons dried parsley
½	teaspoon black pepper
½	teaspoon salt
2	tablespoons chopped fresh dill or parsley

In a large saucepan, heat the oil over medium heat. Add the onion, leeks, and garlic and cook, stirring, for 5 to 7 minutes. Add the water, beets, potatoes, wine, parsley, pepper, and salt and bring to a simmer over medium-high heat. Reduce the heat to medium-low and cook, stirring occasionally, until the beets are tender, 40 to 45 minutes. Remove from the heat and stir in the dill.

Transfer the soup to a food processor fitted with a steel blade (or to a blender) and process until smooth, 5 to 10 seconds. Return the soup to the pan and keep hot over low heat until ready to serve.

To serve, ladle the soup into bowls. Garnish each bowl with a sprig of leftover herbs.

Succotash Squash Soup

Green lima beans and corn are a natural duo in this brightly flavored, wintry soup.

Yield: 8 servings

1	tablespoon canola oil
1	medium yellow onion, diced
1	green or red bell pepper, seeded and diced
2	stalks celery, chopped
2	or 3 cloves garlic, minced
4	cups water
3	cups peeled, diced butternut squash
2	tablespoons dried parsley
2	teaspoons ground cumin
¾	teaspoon salt
½	teaspoon black pepper
1	package (10 ounces) frozen green lima beans (about 2 cups)
1	can (14 ounces) corn, drained

In a large saucepan, heat the oil over medium heat. Add the onion, bell pepper, celery, and garlic and cook, stirring, for 7 minutes. Add the water, squash, parsley, cumin, salt, and pepper and bring to a simmer over medium-high heat. Reduce the heat to medium-low and cook until the squash is tender, about 20 minutes, stirring occasionally. Add the lima beans and corn and cook for 10 to 15 minutes, stirring occasionally.

Remove from the heat and let stand for about 5 minutes. To thicken, mash the squash against the side of the pan with the back of a spoon.

Ladle the soup into bowls and serve at once.

Haitian Hot Pot

This Caribbean melting pot is a molten cauldron of hearty squash, potatoes, turnips, red beans, and fiery hot peppers.

Yield: 8 servings

1	tablespoon canola oil
1	medium yellow onion, diced
1	large green or red bell pepper, seeded and diced
1	stalk celery, diced
2	cloves garlic, minced
½	Scotch bonnet or 2 large jalapeño chili peppers, seeded and minced
8	cups water
2	cups peeled, diced butternut squash or West Indian pumpkin
1	large white potato, peeled and diced
1	medium turnip, peeled and diced
1	tablespoon dried parsley
1	teaspoon dried thyme
1	teaspoon salt
¼	teaspoon ground turmeric
1	can (15 ounces) red kidney beans, drained

In a large saucepan, heat the oil over medium heat. Add the onion, bell pepper, celery, garlic, and chili pepper and cook, stirring, for 5 to 7 minutes. Add the water, squash, potato, turnip, parsley, thyme, salt, and turmeric and bring to a simmer over high heat. Reduce the heat to medium-low and cook for about 45 minutes, stirring occasionally. Stir in the beans and cook for about 5 minutes. To thicken, mash the squash and potatoes against the side of the pan with the back of a large spoon. Remove the soup from the heat and let stand for about 10 minutes.

Ladle the soup into bowls and serve.

Helpful Tip:

Fresh Scotch bonnet peppers are available in well-stocked supermarkets and Caribbean grocery stores.

West Indian Pumpkin Bisque

Although the Caribbean is famous for mangoes, papayas, and other tropical fruits, it is also the home of the West Indian pumpkin, a huge, hubbard-like squash with a bright orange flesh. This poignant pumpkin soup is scented with curry and ginger root.

Yield: 6 servings

1	tablespoon canola oil
1	medium yellow onion, diced
1	cup sliced celery
4	cloves garlic, minced
2	teaspoons minced fresh ginger root
1	jalapeño or other hot chili pepper, seeded and minced
2	large tomatoes, diced
2	to 3 teaspoons curry powder
1½	teaspoons ground cumin
1	teaspoon salt
½	teaspoon black pepper
¼	teaspoon ground cloves
4	cups peeled, diced West Indian pumpkin or other winter squash
5	cups water

In a large saucepan, heat the oil over medium heat. Add the onion, celery, garlic, ginger, and jalapeño and cook, stirring, for 5 minutes. Add the tomatoes and cook, stirring, for 2 to 3 minutes. Stir in the curry powder, cumin, salt, pepper, and cloves and cook, stirring, for 1 minute over low heat. Add the pumpkin and water and bring to a simmer over high heat. Reduce the heat to medium-low and cook until the pumpkin is tender, about 35 minutes, stirring occasionally.

Transfer the soup to a food processor fitted with a steel blade (or to a blender) and process until smooth, about 5 seconds.

Ladle the soup into bowls and serve at once.

Asian Greens and Tofu Soup

This brothy soup can be made with a variety of healthful Asian leafy greens, such as bok choy, napa, and Chinese cabbage, spinach, or whatever is in season.

Yield: 6 servings

1	tablespoon canola oil
1	medium yellow onion, chopped
2	medium carrots, peeled and slivered at an angle
2	cloves garlic, minced
2	teaspoons minced fresh ginger root
6	cups water or vegetable stock
¼	cup soy sauce
2	teaspoons rice vinegar
1	to 2 teaspoons sesame oil
½	teaspoon black pepper
½	pound extra-firm tofu, cut into ½-inch cubes
2	cups chopped bok choy or spinach
2	cups chopped Chinese cabbage or napa cabbage
1	cup snow pea pods, trimmed and halved

In a large saucepan, heat the oil over medium heat. Add the onion, carrots, garlic, and ginger and cook, stirring, for 5 minutes. Add the water, soy sauce, rice vinegar, sesame oil, and pepper and bring to a simmer over high heat. Reduce the heat to medium-low and cook for about 15 minutes, stirring occasionally. Stir in the tofu, bok choy, cabbage, and snow peas and cook for 10 to 15 minutes, stirring occasionally. Remove from the heat and let stand for 5 to 10 minutes before serving.

Ladle the soup into bowls and serve hot.

Helpful Tip:

To give the soup a woodsy flavor, add 6 to 8 fresh shiitake or oyster mushrooms to the pan while sautéing the onion and carrots.

Mushroom, Barley, and Greens Soup

Everyone seems to have a memory (or recipe) of their favorite mushroom and barley soup. This version is enhanced with dark leafy greens, wine, and a hint of mustard.

Yield: 6 servings

1	tablespoon canola oil
12	ounces button mushrooms, sliced
1	medium yellow onion, diced
2	cloves garlic, minced
6	cups water
2	large carrots, peeled and diced
½	cup pearled barley
¼	cup dry white wine
2	teaspoons Dijon-style mustard
1½	tablespoons dried parsley
1	teaspoon dried thyme
1	teaspoon salt
½	teaspoon black pepper
4	cups coarsely chopped kale, spinach, or green chard

In a large saucepan, heat the oil over medium heat. Add the mushrooms, onion, and garlic and cook, stirring, for 8 to 10 minutes. Add the water, carrots, barley, wine, mustard, parsley, thyme, salt, and pepper and bring to a simmer over high heat. Reduce the heat to low and cook for 50 minutes to 1 hour, stirring occasionally. Stir in the greens and cook for 10 minutes. Remove from the heat and let stand for 5 to 10 minutes before serving.

Ladle the soup into bowls and serve with dark bread.

Wild Mushroom and Barley Soup

Lately, there has been an avalanche of fancy wild mushrooms at the greengrocery. This is a boon for epicures, as exotic mushrooms add woodsy flavors and sturdy textures to a variety of meals—including this nourishing vegetable and barley soup.

Yield: 6 servings

1	tablespoon canola oil
12	ounces white mushrooms, sliced
4	ounces fresh shiitake or oyster mushrooms, sliced
4	ounces Italian brown mushrooms (cremini), sliced
1	medium yellow onion, diced
2	stalks celery, chopped
2	tablespoons chopped shallots
6	cups water
½	cup pearl barley
¼	cup dry white wine
2	teaspoons Dijon-style mustard
2	tablespoons dried parsley
1	teaspoon dried thyme
½	teaspoon salt
½	teaspoon black pepper
⅓	pound green beans, trimmed and cut into 1-inch pieces

In a large saucepan, heat the oil over medium heat. Add the mushrooms, onion, celery, and shallots and cook, stirring, for 8 to 10 minutes. Add the water, barley, wine, mustard, parsley, thyme, salt, and pepper and cook for about 50 minutes over medium-low heat, stirring occasionally. Stir in the green beans and cook for 10 minutes. Remove from the heat and let stand for several minutes before serving.

Ladle the soup into bowls and serve with warm dark bread.

Thai Mushroom Noodle Soup

This soup's delicate coconut flavor is juxtaposed with a strong hint of Thai curry, lime, and lemongrass. Firm-textured portobello mushrooms replace the traditional chicken.

Yield: 3 to 4 servings

1	tablespoon canola or peanut oil
1	small yellow onion, finely chopped
1	small red bell pepper, seeded and chopped
6	ounces portobello mushroom caps or button mushrooms, sliced
1	large clove garlic, minced
2	teaspoons minced fresh lemongrass
1	to 1½ teaspoons Thai panang or green curry paste
1	can (14 ounces) coconut milk
1	cup water
2	tablespoons soy sauce
	Juice of ½ lime
1½	teaspoons cornstarch
1½	teaspoons warm water
½	ounce cellophane or bean thread noodles
2	tablespoons chopped cilantro
2	scallions, chopped

In a large saucepan, heat the oil over medium heat. Add the onion, bell pepper, mushrooms, garlic, and lemongrass and cook, stirring, for 6 to 7 minutes. Stir in the curry paste and cook, stirring, for 1 minute over low heat. Stir in the coconut milk, water, soy sauce, and lime juice and cook for 10 minutes over medium-low heat, stirring occasionally.

In a small mixing bowl, combine the cornstarch and warm water. Whisk the cornstarch mixture into the soup and simmer for 1 minute, stirring frequently. Stir in the noodles and cilantro, return to a simmer over medium heat. Turn off the heat, and let stand on the burner until the noodles are soft and translucent, about 7 to 10 minutes.

Ladle the soup into bowls and garnish with the scallions.

Helpful Tip:

Thai panang curry paste, coconut milk, lemongrass, and cellophane noodles can be found at Asian grocery stores and well-stocked supermarkets.

Mexican Tortilla Soup

Called sopa de tortilla in Spanish, this classic soup is a spicy broth of vegetables, chili peppers, corn, and strips of flour tortillas. It's an excellent way to use up day-old tortillas.

Yield: 6 servings

1	tablespoon canola oil
1	medium yellow onion, diced
1	small zucchini, diced
1	red bell pepper, seeded and diced
2	cloves garlic, minced
1	or 2 jalapeño or serrano chili peppers, seeded and minced
6	cups water or vegetable stock
1	can (14 ounces) stewed tomatoes
2	teaspoons dried oregano
1½	teaspoons ground cumin
1	teaspoon salt
1	can (11 ounces) corn, drained
4	(6-inch) flour tortillas, halved and cut into ½-inch-wide strips
2	to 3 tablespoons chopped fresh cilantro

In a large saucepan, heat the oil over medium heat. Add the onion, zucchini, bell pepper, garlic, and chili pepper and cook, stirring, for 5 to 7 minutes. Add the water, stewed tomatoes, oregano, cumin, and salt and bring to a simmer over medium-high heat. Reduce the heat to low and cook for 15 minutes, stirring occasionally. Stir in the corn and tortilla strips and cook for 10 to 15 minutes. Stir in the cilantro. Remove from the heat and let stand for 5 minutes before serving.

Ladle the soup into bowls and serve at once.

White Bean, Corn, and Eggplant Chili

This Southwestern-style chili has taken our taste buds down a path less traveled, and that has made all the difference.

Yield: 4 servings

1½	tablespoons canola oil
1	large onion, diced
1	red or green bell pepper, seeded and diced
2	cups diced eggplant
2	cloves garlic, minced
2	cups corn kernels, fresh or frozen
1	can (15 ounces) white kidney beans, drained
1	can (14 ounces) stewed tomatoes
2	tablespoons dried parsley
1	tablespoon dried oregano
½	teaspoon salt
½	teaspoon black pepper

In a large saucepan, heat the oil over medium heat. Add the onion, bell pepper, eggplant, and garlic and cook, stirring, until the vegetables are tender, about 10 minutes. Stir in the corn, beans, tomatoes, parsley, oregano, salt, and pepper and cook over low heat for about 20 minutes, stirring frequently. Remove from the heat and let stand for about 5 minutes before serving.

Ladle the soup into bowls and serve with warm bread.

Curried Potato and Green Pea Soup

*This savory soup, scented with coriander and garam masala,
was inspired by the Indian pea soup called hara shorva.*

Yield: 6 servings

1	tablespoon canola oil
1	medium yellow onion, diced
2	cloves garlic, minced
1	serrano or fresh cayenne chili pepper, seeded and minced
2	teaspoons curry powder
1	teaspoon ground cumin
1	teaspoon ground coriander
½	teaspoon garam masala
½	teaspoon salt
6	cups water
4	cups peeled, diced white potatoes
1	large carrot, peeled and diced
2	cups frozen green peas

In a large saucepan, heat the oil over medium heat. Add the
onion, garlic, and chili pepper and cook, stirring, for 4 minutes.
Stir in the curry powder, cumin, coriander, garam masala, and
salt and cook, stirring, for 1 minute over low heat. Add the
water, potatoes, and carrot and cook over medium-low heat

until the potatoes are tender, 20 to 25 minutes, stirring occasionally. Stir in the green peas and cook for 5 to 7 minutes over low heat. Remove from the heat and let stand for 10 minutes.

To thicken, mash some of the potatoes against the side of the pan with the back of a large spoon. You can also puree the soup in a blender and serve as a bisque.

Ladle the soup into bowls and serve.

Helpful Tip:

Garam masala is a spice mixture sold in well-stocked supermarkets and natural food stores.

Wild Rice and Split Pea Soup

Wild rice adds a gentle texture and grassy flavor to this cauldron of split peas and winter vegetables.

Yield: 6 servings

1	tablespoon canola oil
1	large red onion, diced
2	stalks celery, chopped
12	ounces button mushrooms, sliced
2	or 3 large cloves garlic, minced
10	cups water
1	cup green split peas, rinsed
2	large carrots, diced
2	cups peeled, diced white potatoes
½	cup wild rice
2	tablespoons dried parsley
2	teaspoons dried oregano
1	teaspoon black pepper
1	teaspoon salt

In a large saucepan, heat the oil over medium-high heat. Add the onion, celery, mushrooms, and garlic and cook, stirring, for about 7 minutes. Stir in the water, split peas, carrots, potatoes, wild rice, parsley, oregano, and pepper and bring to a simmer over medium-high heat. Reduce the heat to medium-low and cook, uncovered, until the split peas are tender, 1½ to 2 hours, stirring occasionally.

Stir in the salt and cook for 5 minutes. Remove from the heat and let stand for 5 minutes before serving.

Ladle the soup into bowls and serve with bread.

Helpful Tip:

Wild rice is available in natural food stores and well-stocked supermarkets.

Beta "Carrotene" Bisque

This recipe combines carrots and sweet potatoes—two carotenoid-rich vegetables—into one delicious (and nutritious) soup.

Yield: 4 servings

1	tablespoon canola oil
1	medium yellow onion, diced
1	large stalk celery, chopped
2	cloves garlic, minced
4	cups water or vegetable broth
2	cups peeled, diced sweet potatoes
1	cup diced carrots
1	teaspoon ground coriander or cumin
½	teaspoon salt
½	teaspoon black pepper
½	teaspoon curry powder or ground turmeric
1	cup soy milk

In a large saucepan, heat the oil over medium heat. Add the onion, celery, and garlic and cook, stirring, for 5 minutes. Add the water, sweet potatoes, carrots, coriander, salt, pepper, and curry powder and bring to a simmer over high heat. Reduce the heat to medium-low and cook until the sweet potatoes and carrots are tender, 20 to 25 minutes, stirring occasionally.

Transfer the soup to a blender or to a food processor fitted with a steel blade and process until smooth, 5 to 10 seconds. Return the soup to the pan and stir in the soy milk. Gently reheat over low heat if necessary.

Ladle the soup into bowls and serve at once.

Sweet Potato Vichyssoise

Sweet potatoes add a touch of fun (and a burst of flavor) to this classic potato bisque.

Yield: 6 servings

1	tablespoon canola oil
1	medium yellow onion, diced
2	cups chopped leeks, rinsed
2	large cloves garlic, minced
4	cups water or vegetable stock
4	cups peeled, coarsely chopped sweet potatoes
2	medium carrots, diced
¼	cup dry white wine
½	teaspoon salt
½	teaspoon white pepper
3	tablespoons chopped fresh parsley
1	to 2 tablespoons chopped fresh dill
1	cup soy milk

In a large saucepan, heat the oil over medium heat. Add the onion, leeks, and garlic and cook, stirring, for about 5 minutes. Add the water, sweet potatoes, carrots, wine, salt, and pepper and bring to a simmer over high heat. Reduce the heat to medium-low and cook until the potatoes are tender, about 25 minutes, stirring occasionally. Stir in the parsley and dill. Remove from the heat and let sit for about 5 minutes.

Transfer the soup to a blender or to a food processor fitted with a steel blade and process until smooth, 5 to 10 seconds. Return the soup to the pan and stir in the soy milk. Reheat the soup over low heat until it barely simmers.

Ladle the soup into bowls and garnish with extra sprigs of herbs.

Wintry Tomato Vegetable Soup

Any soup that calls for zucchini, mushrooms, tomatoes, and plenty of herbs is destined to be extremely satisfying and flavorful.

Yield: 6 servings

1	tablespoon canola oil
1	medium yellow onion, diced
1	small zucchini, diced
8	to 10 white mushrooms, sliced
3	or 4 cloves garlic, minced
6	cups water
1	can (14 ounces) stewed tomatoes
1	can (6 ounces) tomato paste
1½	tablespoons dried parsley
2	teaspoons dried basil
2	teaspoons dried oregano
1	teaspoon salt
½	teaspoon black pepper
½	cup tubettini, ditalini, or other tiny pasta

In a large saucepan, heat the oil over medium heat. Add the onion, zucchini, mushrooms, and garlic and cook, stirring, for 7 minutes. Add the water, stewed tomatoes, tomato paste, parsley, basil, oregano, salt, and pepper and bring to a simmer over medium-high heat. Reduce the heat to medium-low and cook for 16 to 18 minutes, stirring occasionally. Stir in the pasta and cook until the pasta is al dente, about 12 minutes, stirring occasionally. Remove from the heat and let stand for 5 to 10 minutes before serving.

Ladle the soup into bowls and serve with warm Italian bread.

World Beet Soup

This is a true beet lover's soup. The beets produce an inviting, magenta-hued soup, while the brown rice adds a chewy substance and body.

Yield: 6 to 8 servings

1	tablespoon canola oil
1	medium yellow onion, diced
1	green bell pepper, seeded and diced
2	stalks celery, sliced
2	or 3 cloves garlic, minced
6	cups water
2	cups diced, peeled beets
1	can (14 ounces) stewed tomatoes
½	cup long-grain brown rice
2	teaspoons dried oregano
1	teaspoon dried thyme
1	teaspoon Tabasco or other bottled hot sauce
1	teaspoon salt
½	teaspoon black pepper
2	cups coarsely chopped beet greens or spinach
3	to 4 tablespoons chopped fresh parsley

In a large saucepan, heat the oil over medium heat. Add the onion, bell pepper, celery, and garlic and cook, stirring, for 7 minutes. Stir in the water, beets, tomatoes, rice, oregano, thyme, Tabasco, salt, and pepper and cook over medium-low heat, stirring occasionally, until the beets are tender, 50 minutes to 1 hour. Stir in the beet greens and parsley and cook for 5 to 10 minutes. Remove from the heat and let stand for 10 minutes before serving.

Ladle the soup into bowls and serve with warm corn bread.

Moroccan Lentil and Kale Stew with Sautéed Onions

This tureen of lentils, carrots, and kale will satisfy almost any hungry appetite. As with many traditional Moroccan soups, this stew calls for a squeeze of lemon and is topped with sautéed golden onions.

Yield: 6 servings

1	tablespoon canola oil
2	large carrots, peeled and diced
1	medium yellow onion, diced
2	cloves garlic, minced
7	cups water
1½	cups green lentils, rinsed
2	teaspoons ground cumin
½	teaspoon black pepper
2	cups coarsely chopped kale or spinach
3	or 4 tablespoons chopped fresh parsley
1	teaspoon salt
	Juice of 1 lemon

Sautéed Onions

2   teaspoons olive oil
1   large yellow onion, thinly sliced

In a large saucepan, heat the canola oil over medium-high heat. Add the carrots, diced onion, and garlic and cook, stirring, for 5 minutes. Stir in the water, lentils, cumin, and pepper and bring to a simmer over high heat. Reduce the heat to low and cook, stirring occasionally, until the lentils are tender, 45 to 55 minutes. Stir in the kale, parsley, salt, and lemon juice and cook for 10 to 15 minutes.

Meanwhile, in a large skillet, heat the olive oil over medium heat. Add the sliced onion and cook, stirring, until lightly browned, about 7 minutes.

Ladle the stew into bowls and top each with a portion of the sautéed onions.

Triple-Pepper Chili

This spicy "bowl of red" beckons with bold, piquant flavors. Ancho chilies, jalapeños, and bell peppers provide a gamut of tasty sensations.

Yield: 4 servings

2	large ancho chili peppers
1	tablespoon canola oil
1	medium yellow onion, diced
1	red bell pepper, seeded and diced
1	large stalk celery, chopped
2	large cloves garlic, minced
2	jalapeño chili peppers, seeded and minced
2	cans (15 ounces each) black beans or red kidney beans, drained
1	can (28 ounces) crushed tomatoes
1	tablespoon chili powder
2	teaspoons dried oregano
½	teaspoon salt

Soak the ancho chilies in enough boiling water to cover and set aside for 20 to 25 minutes. Drain the liquid, remove the seeds of the peppers, and chop the pods.

In a large saucepan, heat the oil over medium heat. Add the onion, bell pepper, celery, garlic, and jalapeño and cook, stirring, for 7 minutes. Add the beans, tomatoes, chili powder, oregano, salt, and ancho peppers and bring to a simmer over high heat. Reduce the heat to medium-low and cook for 15 to 20 minutes, stirring occasionally.

Ladle the chili into bowls and serve with warm bread.

Helpful Tip:

Ancho chilies are anvil-shaped poblano peppers that have been dried. If ancho chilies are unavailable, try another dried pepper, such as chipotle or guajillo.

Pasta e Fagiole

This bountiful Italian soup (pronounced "pasta fazool") is meant to be enjoyed with plenty of napkins and elbow room.

Yield: 8 servings

1	tablespoon olive oil
1	medium yellow onion, diced
1	small yellow summer squash or zucchini, diced
10	to 12 white mushrooms, sliced
3	or 4 cloves garlic, minced
7	cups water
1	can (14 ounces) stewed tomatoes
¼	cup dry red wine
6	tablespoons canned tomato paste
1	tablespoon dried oregano
2	teaspoons dried basil
1	teaspoon salt
½	teaspoon black pepper
½	cup ditalini, tubettini, or soup shells
1	can (15 ounces) cranberry beans or Roman beans, drained
¼	pound green beans, trimmed and cut into 1-inch pieces

In a large saucepan, heat the oil over medium heat. Add the onion, squash, mushrooms, and garlic and cook, stirring, for 7 minutes. Add the water, tomatoes, wine, tomato paste, oregano, basil, salt, and pepper and bring to a simmer over high heat. Reduce the heat to medium-low and cook for 20 to 25 minutes, stirring occasionally.

Stir in the pasta, beans, and green beans and cook until the pasta is al dente, 12 to 15 minutes. Occasionally stir the soup while it cooks. Remove from the heat and let sit for 10 minutes before serving.

Ladle the soup into bowls and serve with warm Italian bread.

Helpful Tips:

If fresh herbs are available, add 2 to 3 tablespoons of chopped fresh basil or arugula at the finish. Ditalini and tubettini are tiny pastas, available in the pasta section of most grocery stores.

Sizzling
Black Bean Soup

*For as long as I have been a chef, I have loved black bean soups.
The legumes have an earthy, inviting flavor and meld easily
into vegetable broths, stews, and chilies.*

Yield: 6 servings

1½	cups dried black beans, soaked overnight and drained
6	cups water
1	tablespoon canola oil
1	large yellow onion, diced
1	green or red bell pepper, seeded and diced
1	large stalk celery, chopped
3	or 4 cloves garlic, minced
1	large jalapeño chili pepper, seeded and minced
2	medium carrots, peeled and diced
2	to 3 tablespoons minced fresh parsley
1	tablespoon dried oregano
1½	teaspoons ground cumin
1	teaspoon ground coriander
1	teaspoon dried thyme
½	teaspoon black pepper
½	cup canned crushed tomatoes
1	teaspoon salt
2	tablespoons chopped fresh cilantro

In a large saucepan, combine the beans and 6 cups water and
bring to a simmer over medium-high heat. Cook over medium-
low heat until the beans are tender, 1 to 1½ hours. Drain the
beans, reserving 4 cups of the cooking liquid.

In a large saucepan, heat the oil over medium heat. Add the onion, bell pepper, celery, garlic, and jalapeño and cook, stirring, for 6 minutes. Add the beans and reserved cooking liquid, carrots, parsley, oregano, cumin, coriander, thyme, and pepper and bring to a simmer over high heat. Reduce the heat to medium-low and cook for about 20 minutes, stirring occasionally. Stir in the tomatoes, salt, and cilantro and cook for 10 minutes, stirring occasionally.

Remove from the heat and let stand for 5 to 10 minutes before serving. If you prefer a thicker soup, puree half of the mixture in a food processor fitted with a steel blade (or in a blender) and return to the pan.

Ladle the soup into bowls. Serve with warm flour tortillas.

Helpful Tip:

Soak the beans in plenty of water before cooking. Soaking yields a fuller, plumper bean and reduces the cooking time. After draining, cook the beans in fresh water.

Jay's Mondo Chili

A salubrious bowl of hot chili takes the bite out of a harsh, wintry day. This is one of my favorite antidotes to the cold-weather blues.

Yield: 4 servings

1	tablespoon canola oil
1	large yellow onion, diced
1	green bell pepper, seeded and diced
1	red bell pepper, seeded and diced
1	cup sliced celery
2	large cloves garlic, minced
1	can (28 ounces) crushed tomatoes
1	can (15 ounces) red kidney beans, drained
1	can (14 ounces) stewed tomatoes, diced
1½	to 2 tablespoons chili powder
1	tablespoon dried oregano
2½	teaspoons ground cumin
1	teaspoon paprika
1	teaspoon salt
1	to 2 teaspoons Tabasco or other bottled hot sauce
½	teaspoon black pepper

In a large saucepan, heat the oil over medium heat. Add the onion, green and red bell pepper, celery, and garlic and cook, stirring, for 7 minutes. Stir in the crushed tomatoes, beans, stewed tomatoes, chili powder, oregano, cumin, paprika, salt, Tabasco, and pepper and bring to a simmer over medium-high heat. Reduce the heat to medium-low and cook for 20 minutes, stirring occasionally. Remove from the heat and let stand for 5 minutes.

Ladle the chili into bowls and serve with warm bread.

Chapter 2

⊨◇⊣

Salads, Greens, and Some Beans

$\mathcal{A}$ simple salad can be a wonderful thing. Depending on your mood or appetite, a salad can serve as a stimulating appetizer, a light entree, or a cleanser for a satisfied palate. Perhaps the salad is an unintimidating plate of leafy greens lightly dressed with a tangy vinaigrette, or it's a bowl of pasta, chick-peas, and asparagus coated with an herbal dressing. It could be a combination of brown rice, black beans, corn, and scallions tossed with a citrus marinade, or it could be roasted beets blended with baby potatoes. A variety of well-made salads plays an important role in the healthful vegan diet.

This chapter offers a plethora of recipes for artful salads, leafy greens, and bean salads, from Tropical Black Bean and Rice Salad, Santa Fe Pasta Salad, and Lemony Whole Grain Salad to Mesclun Salad Bowl and Lemon-Braised Market Greens. This is a compendium of light and healthful salad entrees prepared with a medley of greens, vegetables, grains, beans, and pastas—and all are easy to prepare and a joy to devour.

This chapter also highlights a variety of dark leafy greens that can be quickly cooked and served as a warm salad or side dish. Sturdy greens such as kale, green chard, spinach, and frisée add a touch of panache to the meal and are easy to prepare. Braised leafy greens are also loaded with disease-fighting antioxidants, phytochemicals, and vitamins and are welcome staples in the heart-healthy kitchen. (As a general rule, the darker the leaf, the more vitamins and minerals are present.)

Of course, salads are not limited to leafy green vegetables. Grains, beans, and pastas form the foundation of many salads, while garden vegetables add alluring colors and flavor. Beets, carrots, green beans, summer squash, and other healthy staples are welcome in the new *garde-manger*. Mustard, horseradish, garlic, and chilies provide depth and diversity, while vinegar, citrus juice, and herbs all add a boost of flavor—with few calories or fat.

Tropical Black Bean and Rice Salad

Black beans and rice, together forever. Long-grain rice or parboiled rice are a good choice for salads because of their "fluffy" texture.

Yield: 6 servings

2	cans (15 ounces each) black beans, drained
2	cups cooked long-grain white rice or parboiled rice
4	whole scallions, trimmed and chopped
2	medium tomatoes, diced
1	cucumber, peeled and diced
1	large jalapeño chili pepper, seeded and minced
3	tablespoons canola oil
	Juice of 1½ to 2 limes
2	to 3 tablespoons chopped fresh cilantro
2	teaspoons dried oregano
1	teaspoon ground cumin
½	teaspoon black pepper
½	teaspoon salt

In a large mixing bowl, combine the beans, rice, scallions, tomatoes, cucumber, chili pepper, oil, lime juice, cilantro, oregano, cumin, pepper, and salt and mix thoroughly. Chill the salad for 30 minutes to 1 hour to allow the flavors to meld.

If desired, serve over a bed of leafy green lettuce.

Helpful Tip:

If cilantro is unavailable, add about ¼ cup chopped fresh parsley.

Asian Noodles with Peanut Dressing

Rice vermicelli are thin white noodles with a mild rice flavor. They cook up quickly and are great for salads and cold dishes.

Yield: 4 servings

3	quarts plus 2 tablespoons water
8	ounces rice vermicelli
¼	cup plus 2 tablespoons chunky peanut butter
¼	cup low-sodium soy sauce
2	tablespoons mirin (rice wine)
2	teaspoons minced fresh ginger root
¼	pound extra-firm tofu, diced (preferably roasted)
4	whole scallions, trimmed and chopped
½	cup diced roasted red bell peppers
½	cup slivered water chestnuts
2	tablespoons chopped fresh cilantro

In a large saucepan, bring 3 quarts of water to a boil. Add the vermicelli and cook over medium heat until it is al dente, about 5 minutes, stirring occasionally. Drain in a colander and cool under cold running water.

In a medium mixing bowl, whisk the peanut butter, soy sauce, mirin, 2 tablespoons water, and ginger. Add the cooked noodles, tofu, scallions, roasted peppers, water chestnuts, and cilantro and blend.

Serve the noodles warm or refrigerate for later.

Helpful Tips:

Mirin is a sweetened rice wine and can be found in Asian markets and well-stocked supermarkets. Roasted red bell peppers may be found in jars in the relish/pickle section of grocery stores. Roasted or baked tofu is available in natural food stores and well-stocked supermarkets.

Santa Fe Pasta Salad

The flavors of the Southwestern kitchen—lime, cilantro, cumin, and jalapeño—infuse this pasta salad with a lighthearted flair.

Yield: 6 servings

2½	quarts water
8	ounces pasta spirals or penne
2	tablespoons canola oil
	Juice of 2 limes
¼	cup chopped fresh cilantro
3	or 4 cloves garlic, minced
1	or 2 jalapeño chili peppers, seeded and minced
1½	teaspoons ground cumin
½	teaspoon black pepper
½	teaspoon salt
2	tomatoes, diced
1	can (15 ounces) black beans, drained
1	can (11 ounces) corn kernels, drained
4	whole scallions, trimmed and chopped
1	green bell pepper, seeded and diced

In a large saucepan, bring the water to a boil over medium-high heat. Add the pasta, stir, and return to a boil. Reduce the heat to medium and cook until the pasta is al dente, 10 to 12 minutes, stirring occasionally. Drain the pasta in a colander and cool under cold running water.

In a large mixing bowl, whisk the oil, lime juice, cilantro, garlic, jalapeño, cumin, pepper, and salt. Stir in the pasta, tomatoes, beans, corn, scallions, and bell pepper. Refrigerate the salad for 30 minutes to 1 hour before serving to allow the flavors to meld. Fluff the salad before serving.

Mizuna Salad with Caramelized Onions

Lightly browned onions have a warm, comforting, almost sweet flavor. In this dish, the cooked onions bring out the mustardlike nuance of mizuna greens, a frilly Japanese leafy vegetable. Serve the greens as a first course or side dish.

Yield: 4 servings

1	tablespoon canola oil
2	medium yellow onions, cut into thin strips
1	large red bell pepper, seeded and cut into thin strips
1	tablespoon balsamic vinegar
1	tablespoon brown sugar
1	bunch mizuna greens, rinsed and coarsely chopped
2	ounces alfalfa sprouts
1	tomato, cut into wedges

In a large skillet, heat the oil over medium-high heat. Add the onions and bell pepper and cook, stirring, until the onions are lightly browned, about 7 minutes. Reduce the heat to low and stir in the vinegar and sugar. Cook, stirring, for 2 minutes.

Arrange the mizuna greens, sprouts, and tomato on salad plates. Using tongs, place the onion mixture over the top of each plate.

Helpful Tip:

Mizuna greens are available on a seasonal basis (usually in late summer and spring) at natural food stores and farmers' markets.

Mesclun Salad Bowl

Mesclun is the French term for "mixed field greens." Young, tender leafy greens make the best mesclun salad. Try a variety of leafy greens, such as red leaf lettuce, watercress, arugula, mâche, red chard, beet greens, and mizuna.

Yield: 4 servings

6	to 8 cups mixed leafy greens, rinsed and torn into bite-sized shapes
10	to 12 cherry tomatoes, halved
1	small red onion, cut into thin strips
1	small cucumber, sliced
2	medium carrots, peeled and shredded
½	cup alfalfa or mung bean sprouts
1	cup canned chick-peas, drained
	Balsamic vinegar or your favorite dressing, to taste

Place the greens in the center of a large salad bowl and arrange the tomatoes, onion, cucumber, carrots, and sprouts around the edge. Sprinkle the chick-peas over the center. Drizzle the vinegar over the greens and vegetables.

Serve the salad on small plates with crusty French bread.

Jicama, Avocado, and Bean Salad

Jicama, also called Mexican potato, adds a nice crunchiness to this lightly dressed two-bean and avocado salad.

Yield: 6 servings

1	can (15 ounces) black beans, drained
1	can (15 ounces) red kidney beans, drained
2	ripe avocados, peeled, pitted, and diced
2	medium tomatoes, diced
1	cup peeled, diced jicama
2	whole scallions, chopped
1	red or green bell pepper, seeded and diced
2	large cloves garlic, minced
	Juice of 1 large lime
2	tablespoons chopped fresh cilantro
2	teaspoons dried oregano
1	teaspoon ground cumin
½	teaspoon black pepper
½	teaspoon salt

In a mixing bowl, combine the two types of beans, avocados, tomatoes, jicama, scallions, bell pepper, garlic, lime juice, cilantro, oregano, cumin, pepper, and salt and toss thoroughly. Chill until ready to serve.

Serve over a bed of leaf lettuce.

Helpful Tip:
Other beans, such as white kidney beans or chick-peas, can also be used.

Tangy Couscous with Black Beans and Corn

If your supper hour is more like rush hour, then you'll appreciate this easy-to-prepare couscous salad. Serve the salad as a light side dish or filling for a pita sandwich.

Yield: 4 servings

1	cup couscous
1½	cups boiling water
2	tomatoes, diced
1	red or green bell pepper, seeded and diced
4	whole scallions, chopped
1	can (15 ounces) black beans, drained
1	can (14 ounces) corn kernels, drained
2	tablespoons chopped fresh cilantro
½	teaspoon salt
½	teaspoon black pepper
	Juice of 1 large lime

Combine the couscous and boiling water in a bowl or pan, cover, and let stand for about 10 minutes. Fluff the couscous with a fork.

In a medium mixing bowl, combine the couscous with the tomatoes, bell pepper, scallions, beans, corn, cilantro, salt, pepper, and lime juice and toss thoroughly. Chill for 30 minutes before serving.

Somen Noodles with Spicy Peanut Sauce

For this nifty salad, thin somen noodles are tossed with a piquant peanut-soy dressing. Somen noodles are a favorite pasta in Japanese cuisine.

Yield: 3 to 4 servings

2	quarts water
8	ounces somen noodles or rice vermicelli
¼	cup chunky peanut butter
¼	cup warm water
2	tablespoons soy sauce
1	tablespoon rice vinegar
1	teaspoon sesame oil
1	teaspoon hot sesame oil
2	large cloves garlic, minced
1	large red Fresno or jalapeño chili pepper, seeded and minced
¼	teaspoon ground cayenne
4	whole scallions, trimmed and chopped

In a large saucepan, bring the water to a boil. Add the noodles, stir, and cook over medium heat until al dente, 3 to 5 minutes. Drain the noodles in a colander and cool under cold running water.

In a mixing bowl, whisk the peanut butter, warm water, soy sauce, rice vinegar, and sesame oils. Blend in the garlic, chili pepper, and cayenne. Toss the noodles with the peanut dressing and chill for about 30 minutes before serving.

Serve the noodles on a bed of lettuce and sprinkle the scallions over the top.

Roasted Beet Salad

Roasting is an easy and painless way to cook beets. Simply wrap them in foil and bake them like a potato. Once cooked, the beets are ready to be tossed with a light dressing and served warm or chilled.

Yield: 4 servings

6	to 8 medium beets, scrubbed and rinsed
3	to 4 tablespoons canola oil
3	tablespoons red wine vinegar
2	teaspoons prepared horseradish
1	teaspoon Dijon-style mustard
1	teaspoon brown sugar
¼	cup chopped mixture of fresh parsley, dill, and basil
½	teaspoon black pepper
½	teaspoon salt

Preheat the oven to 375 degrees F.

Wrap the beets in aluminum foil and place on a baking pan. Roast the beets until they are tender, 50 minutes to 1 hour. Remove the beets from the oven, unwrap, and let cool.

Meanwhile, in a medium mixing bowl, whisk the oil, vinegar, horseradish, mustard, sugar, herb mixture, pepper, and salt. Set aside.

When the beets are cool enough to handle, peel off the loose skins. Coarsely chop the beets and add to the vinaigrette, coating the beets thoroughly. Let stand for 30 minutes and serve warm or refrigerate for later.

Garden Fattoush

This Middle Eastern "bread salad" is a resourceful way to use leftover pita bread.

Yield: 4 servings

2	tablespoons olive oil
1	medium red onion, diced
2	cups diced pita bread (day-old is fine)
2	medium tomatoes, diced
1	cucumber, peeled and chopped
¼	cup chopped fresh parsley
	Juice of 1 large lemon
½	teaspoon black pepper
½	teaspoon salt

In a large skillet, heat the oil over medium heat. Add the onion and cook, stirring, for 4 minutes. Add the bread and cook, stirring, for 5 to 7 minutes. Transfer to a salad bowl and toss with the tomatoes, cucumber, parsley, lemon juice, pepper, and salt.

Spoon the salad onto plates and serve at once.

Grilled Tunisian Vegetable Salad

Grilled vegetable salads are a favorite fixture in North African cuisine. The vegetables are flavored with lemon, olive oil, and a touch of cumin and capers.

Yield: 3 to 4 servings

2	tablespoons olive oil
	Juice of 1 lemon
2	cloves garlic, minced
2	to 3 tablespoons chopped parsley
1	tablespoon capers, rinsed
1	large jalapeño chili pepper, seeded and minced
½	teaspoon ground cumin
2	green bell peppers, seeded and halved
2	red bell peppers, seeded and halved
2	large tomatoes, halved
1	medium red onion, peeled and quartered
4	to 5 cups cooked couscous

Preheat the grill until the coals are gray to white.

In a large mixing bowl, combine the oil, lemon juice, garlic, parsley, capers, jalapeño, and cumin. Set aside.

When the fire is ready, place the vegetables on the grill. Cook until the vegetables are tender (not charred), about 10 minutes. Using tongs, occasionally turn the vegetables as they cook.

Remove the vegetables from the grill and place them on a cutting board. Using a butter knife, scrape off any charred parts. Coarsely chop all of the vegetables and toss with the oil-lemon mixture. Let stand for 5 to 10 minutes.

To serve, spoon the couscous onto serving plates and place the grilled vegetables over the top.

Lemony Artichoke and Rice Salad

Lemon lends a citrusy touch to this salad of vegetables, rice, and garden herbs.

Yield: 4 servings

½	pound green beans, cut into 1-inch pieces
1	can (14 ounces) artichoke hearts, rinsed and quartered
4	cups cooked long-grain white rice or brown rice
4	whole scallions, trimmed and chopped
2	medium tomatoes, diced
1	small cucumber, peeled and diced
3	tablespoons olive oil
	Juice of 2 lemons
¼	cup chopped fresh parsley
2	or 3 tablespoons chopped fresh basil
1	teaspoon salt
½	teaspoon black pepper

Place the green beans in boiling water to cover and cook over high heat until tender, about 3 minutes (you can also steam the beans). Cool the beans in a colander under cold running water.

In a large mixing bowl, combine the beans, artichokes, rice, scallions, tomatoes, and cucumber. In a separate bowl, whisk the oil, lemon juice, parsley, basil, salt, and pepper. Toss the dressing into the rice mixture and chill for about 1 hour before serving to allow the flavors to meld.

To serve, fluff the salad with a fork and serve over a bed of leaf lettuce.

Wild Rice and Quinoa Salad

Wild rice, a native grain of North America, is united with quinoa, an ancient grain of South America. It is a match made in heaven.

Yield: 4 servings

½	cup wild rice
3½	cups water
1	cup quinoa, rinsed
3	or 4 whole scallions, trimmed and chopped
2	or 3 cloves garlic, minced
½	cup roasted sweet peppers, diced
3	tablespoons canola oil
1	tablespoon red wine vinegar
2	to 3 tablespoons chopped fresh parsley
1	teaspoon dried thyme
1	teaspoon Dijon-style mustard
½	teaspoon black pepper
½	teaspoon salt

In a medium saucepan, combine the wild rice and 1½ cups of the water and bring to a simmer over medium-high heat. Stir the grains, cover, and cook over medium-low heat until the rice is tender, 40 to 45 minutes. Fluff and set aside.

Meanwhile, in another medium saucepan, combine the quinoa and the remaining 2 cups of water and bring to a simmer over medium-high heat. Stir the grains, cover, and cook over medium-low heat until all of the water is absorbed, about 15 minutes. Fluff and set aside.

In a large mixing bowl, combine the wild rice, quinoa, scallions, garlic, roasted peppers, oil, vinegar, parsley, thyme, mustard, pepper, and salt. Chill the salad for at least 1 hour before serving.

Helpful Tips:

Quinoa and wild rice are available in natural food stores and well-stocked supermarkets. Remember to first rinse the quinoa in cold water (to wash away the natural, bitter-tasting resin that coats the grains). Roasted sweet peppers are available in jars in the relish/pickle section of grocery stores.

Javanese Tofu, Rice, and Peanut Salad

Roasted tofu adds a chewy texture to this salad of rice and vegetables. A peanut dressing flavored with cilantro and mint strikes just the right chord.

Yield: 4 servings

½	pound extra-firm tofu, cut into ½-inch cubes
¼	cup hot water
3	tablespoons chunky peanut butter
2	to 3 tablespoons low-sodium soy sauce
1	tablespoon rice vinegar
2	cloves garlic, minced
1	jalapeño or serrano chili pepper, seeded and minced
1	teaspoon sesame oil
2	tablespoons chopped fresh mint
2	tablespoons chopped fresh cilantro
3	cups cooked long-grain white rice or brown rice
1	red bell pepper, seeded and diced
3	or 4 whole scallions, trimmed and chopped
1	can (4 ounces) sliced water chestnuts, drained

Preheat the oven to 375 degrees F.

Place the tofu on a lightly greased baking pan and roast until lightly browned, 15 to 20 minutes (stir the tofu after 10 minutes). Remove the pan from the oven and let cool slightly.

Meanwhile, in a large mixing bowl, whisk the water, peanut butter, soy sauce, rice vinegar, garlic, chili pepper, sesame oil, mint, and cilantro. Stir in the rice, bell pepper, scallions, water chestnuts, and tofu, coating the grains and vegetables completely with the dressing. Chill for 30 minutes to 1 hour before serving to allow the flavors to meld.

Fluff the salad before serving over a bed of lettuce. Garnish with any remaining sprigs of herbs.

Lemony Whole Grain Salad

If you can't make up your mind about which type of rice to eat, try a blend of whole grain rices. There are a variety of exotic blends to choose from.

Yield: 6 servings

1	cup whole grain rice blend
2½	cups water
1	can (15 ounces) black beans, drained
1	can (11 ounces) corn kernels, drained
2	medium tomatoes, diced
1	cucumber, peeled and diced
2	tablespoons canola oil
	Juice of 2 lemons
¼	cup chopped fresh parsley
2	teaspoons dried oregano
½	teaspoon black pepper
½	teaspoon salt

In a medium saucepan, combine the rice blend and water and bring to a simmer over medium-high heat. Stir the grains, cover, and cook over medium-low heat until all of the liquid is absorbed, about 30 minutes. Remove from the heat and fluff the grains. Let stand for 5 to 10 minutes.

Meanwhile, in a large mixing bowl, combine the beans, corn, tomatoes, cucumber, oil, lemon juice, parsley, oregano, pepper, and salt and toss thoroughly. Stir in the warm rice. Chill the salad for 1 hour before serving to allow the flavors to meld.

Confetti Quinoa Salad

Nutrient-dense quinoa forms a healthy foundation for this colorful salad of beans, corn, peppers, and lime.

Yield: 4 servings

1	cup quinoa, rinsed
2	cups water
1	can (15 ounces) red kidney beans, drained
4	whole scallions, trimmed and chopped
1	red bell pepper, seeded and diced
1	jalapeño chili pepper, seeded and minced
1	can (14 ounces) corn kernels, drained
2	tablespoons canola oil
2	tablespoons chopped fresh parsley
½	teaspoon black pepper
½	teaspoon salt
2	limes, cut into wedges

In a medium saucepan, combine the quinoa and water and bring to a simmer. Stir the grains, cover, and cook over medium heat until all of the liquid is absorbed, 15 to 18 minutes. Fluff the grains and set aside for 5 minutes.

Meanwhile, in a medium mixing bowl, combine the beans, scallions, bell pepper, jalapeño, corn, oil, parsley, pepper, and salt. Stir in the cooked quinoa and squeeze half of the limes into the salad.

Serve the salad warm or refrigerate for later. Squeeze the remaining lime over the top just before serving.

Helpful Tip:

Quinoa is available in natural food stores and well-stocked supermarkets. Remember to first rinse the quinoa in cold water (to wash away the natural, bitter-tasting resin that coats the grains).

Two-Bean Salad with Corn and Artichokes

This quick-and-easy bean salad is spruced up with mellow balsamic vinegar and a medley of herbs.

Yield: 6 servings

1	can (15 ounces) chick-peas, drained
1	can (15 ounces) red kidney beans or black-eyed peas, drained
1	can (14 ounces) artichoke hearts, drained and coarsely chopped
4	whole scallions, trimmed and chopped
2	large tomatoes, diced
1	can (11 ounces) corn kernels, drained
3	or 4 cloves garlic, minced
2	tablespoons olive oil
2	to 3 tablespoons balsamic vinegar
¼	cup chopped fresh parsley
2	teaspoons dried oregano
½	teaspoon black pepper
½	teaspoon salt

In a large mixing bowl, combine the chick-peas, beans, artichoke, scallions, tomatoes, corn, garlic, oil, vinegar, parsley, oregano, pepper, and salt and blend well. Refrigerate the salad for at least 30 minutes to 1 hour to allow the flavors to meld together. (The salad may be made up to a day ahead of time.)

Serve the salad over a bed of leaf lettuce.

Black-Eyed Pea and Bulgur Salad

You can also serve this healthy bean-and-grain combination as a stuffing for pita bread or light side dish.

Yield: 4 servings

1	cup bulgur
1	cup boiling water
1	can (15 ounces) black-eyed peas, drained
1	large tomato, diced
1	medium cucumber, peeled and diced
2	or 3 large whole scallions, trimmed and chopped
2	cloves garlic, minced
2	tablespoons olive oil
	Juice of 1 to 2 lemons
¼	cup chopped fresh parsley
½	teaspoon black pepper
½	teaspoon salt

In a medium mixing bowl, combine the bulgur and water. Let stand, covered, until the bulgur absorbs all of the water, about 20 minutes. Fluff the grains.

Meanwhile, in another mixing bowl, combine the black-eyed peas, tomato, cucumber, scallions, garlic, oil, lemon juice, parsley, pepper, and salt and toss. Stir the soaked bulgur into the black-eyed pea mixture. Chill the salad for at least 1 hour before serving.

Serve the salad over a bed of leaf lettuce.

Garden
Three-Bean Salad

The classic three-bean salad is reinvigorated with fresh vegetables, garden herbs, and a zesty balsamic vinaigrette.

Yield: 4 to 6 servings

1	can (15 ounces) chick-peas, drained
1	can (15 ounces) red kidney beans, drained
1	can (15 ounces) black beans or black-eyed peas, drained
1	red bell pepper, seeded and diced
1	large cucumber, peeled and diced
4	to 6 whole scallions, trimmed and chopped
2	medium tomatoes, diced
4	cloves garlic, minced
3	tablespoons olive oil
3	tablespoons balsamic vinegar
¼	cup chopped fresh parsley
2	teaspoons dried oregano
1	teaspoon black pepper
½	teaspoon salt

In a large mixing bowl, combine the chick-peas, red and black beans, bell pepper, cucumber, scallions, tomatoes, garlic, oil, vinegar, parsley, oregano, pepper, and salt and blend thoroughly. Chill the salad for at least 1 hour before serving.

Transfer to a large serving bowl and serve over a bed of leaf lettuce.

Helpful Tip:

Blend in 2 to 3 tablespoons of chopped garden herbs, such as basil, arugula, or chives.

Gourmet Potato and Beet Salad

Potato salad is rejuvenated with the addition of beets, herbs, and sunflower seeds. For a taste of diversity, try a gourmet potato such as Yukon gold, fingerling, or baby purple.

Yield: 4 servings

4	or 5 medium beets, scrubbed
2	cups diced Yukon gold or other exotic potato
2	tablespoons canola oil
2	tablespoons apple cider vinegar
1	tablespoon prepared horseradish
1	tablespoon Dijon-style mustard
2	tablespoons chopped fresh dill or parsley
½	teaspoon black pepper
½	teaspoon salt
2	stalks celery, diced
1	medium red onion, finely chopped
3	to 4 tablespoons sunflower seeds

Preheat the oven to 400 degrees F.

Wrap the beets in aluminum foil and place on a baking pan. Roast the beets until tender, 50 minutes to 1 hour. Remove the beets from the oven, unwrap, and let cool. Slip off the skins and coarsely chop the beets.

Meanwhile, in a medium saucepan, place the diced potato in boiling water to cover. Cook over medium-high heat until the potatoes are tender, about 15 minutes. Drain and cool under cold running water.

In a mixing bowl, whisk the oil, vinegar, horseradish, mustard, dill, pepper, and salt. Add the beets, potatoes, celery, onion, and sunflower seeds and blend. Chill for at least 1 hour before serving.

Penne Pasta and Artichoke Salad

Penne has a narrow, tubular shape and makes an excellent choice for a tossed pasta salad. Similar-shaped ziti can also be used.

Yield: 4 servings

2½	quarts water
8	ounces penne or ziti pasta
3	tablespoons canola oil
3	tablespoons red wine vinegar or balsamic vinegar
1	tablespoon Dijon-style mustard
¼	cup chopped fresh parsley
2	large cloves garlic, minced
2	teaspoons dried oregano
½	teaspoon black pepper
2	tomatoes, diced
4	whole scallions, trimmed and chopped
1	can (15 ounces) chick-peas, drained
1	can (14 ounces) artichoke hearts, rinsed and coarsely chopped

In a large saucepan, bring the water to a boil over medium-high heat. Add the pasta, stir, and return to a boil. Cook over medium heat until al dente, 9 to 11 minutes. Drain in a colander and cool under cold running water.

In a large mixing bowl, whisk the oil, vinegar, mustard, parsley, garlic, oregano, and pepper. Add the pasta, tomatoes, scallions, chick-peas, and artichokes and blend. Refrigerate the salad for about 1 hour before serving.

Helpful Tip:

Toss in a green vegetable, such as steamed asparagus, broccoli, or green beans.

Bow-Tie Pasta with Balsamic Herb Vinaigrette

Bow-tie pasta (also called farfalle) is jazzed up with a dressing of balsamic vinegar, fresh herbs, and garden vegetables.

Yield: 6 servings

2½	quarts water
8	ounces bow-tie pasta
3	to 4 tablespoons canola oil
3	tablespoons balsamic vinegar
2	teaspoons Dijon-style mustard
2	large cloves garlic, minced
½	cup mixture of chopped fresh herbs (such as parsley, basil, and oregano)
2	teaspoons dried oregano
½	teaspoon black pepper
½	teaspoon salt
12	to 14 cherry tomatoes, halved
4	whole scallions, trimmed and chopped
1	yellow or red bell pepper, seeded and diced
2	cups coarsely chopped spinach
1	can (15 ounces) chick-peas, drained

In a large saucepan, bring the water to a boil over medium-high heat. Add the pasta, stir, and return to a boil. Cook over medium heat until al dente, 10 to 12 minutes, stirring occasionally. Drain the pasta in a colander and cool under cold running water.

In a large mixing bowl, whisk the oil, vinegar, mustard, garlic, herb mixture, oregano, pepper, and salt. Add the cooked pasta, tomatoes, scallions, bell pepper, spinach, and chick-peas and blend. Refrigerate the salad for about 1 hour before serving.

Wheat Garden Salad

This Middle Eastern favorite should be part of every vegan's culinary repertoire. It can also be served as a stuffing for pita bread.

Yield: 4 servings

1	cup bulgur
1½	cups boiling water
2	large scallions, trimmed and chopped
½	cup chopped fresh parsley
4	plum tomatoes, diced
1	cucumber, peeled and chopped
	Juice of 2 lemons
3	to 4 tablespoons olive oil
½	teaspoon black pepper
½	teaspoon salt

In a medium saucepan, combine the bulgur and water and cover. Let stand until the bulgur absorbs all of the water, about 20 minutes.

In a mixing bowl, combine the bulgur with the scallions, parsley, tomatoes, cucumber, lemon juice, oil, pepper, and salt and toss thoroughly. Chill for 30 minutes to 1 hour before serving.

Serve the salad over a bed of leafy greens.

Lemon–Braised Market Greens

Braising—the method of cooking ingredients in a small amount of liquid—is one of the easiest ways to prepare dark leafy greens. Serve this as a warm salad or side dish.

Yield: 4 servings

1	large bunch kale, Russian kale, or field spinach
1	tablespoon canola oil
1	medium yellow onion, finely chopped
2	cloves garlic, minced
	Juice of 1 large lemon
½	teaspoon black pepper
½	teaspoon salt
1	tablespoon sunflower seeds or sesame seeds

Place the greens in a colander and rinse under cold running water. Remove the stems and coarsely chop the leaves.

In a large skillet, heat the oil over medium heat. Add the onion and garlic and cook, stirring, for 2 to 3 minutes. Add the greens, lemon juice, pepper, and salt and cook over medium-low heat until the greens are wilted, about 5 minutes.

Using tongs, transfer the greens to a shallow serving platter. Sprinkle the seeds over the top and serve.

Tuscan Greens and White Beans

Beans and greens are a dynamic duo. For this Italian dish, a mild green such as escarole is commonly used, but feel free to use almost any leafy green vegetable. Serve it as a warm salad or side dish.

Yield: 4 servings

1	tablespoon olive oil
1	medium yellow onion, chopped
2	or 3 cloves garlic, minced
4	cups coarsely chopped escarole, spinach, or kale
3	tablespoons dry white wine
1	teaspoon ground sage
½	teaspoon salt
¼	teaspoon dried red pepper flakes
1	can (15 ounces) white or red kidney beans, drained
¼	cup chopped fresh basil

In a large saucepan, heat the oil over medium-high heat. Add the onion and garlic and cook, stirring, for 4 minutes. Add the escarole, wine, sage, salt, and red pepper flakes and cook over medium-low heat, stirring frequently, until the greens are wilted, about 5 minutes. Stir in the beans and basil and cook for 3 minutes, stirring occasionally.

Remove from the heat and serve.

Wine-Braised Kale with Wild Mushrooms

Green kale makes a nutritious companion to earthy wild mushrooms. Other greens, such as red Russian kale, escarole, or amaranth greens, can also be used. Serve this as a warm salad or side dish.

Yield: 4 servings

1	medium bunch kale (about 1 pound)
1	tablespoon olive oil
3	tablespoons dry white wine
8	ounces button mushrooms, sliced
4	ounces wild mushrooms (such as cremini, oyster, or shiitake), sliced
1	medium red onion, diced
2	or 3 large cloves garlic, minced
½	teaspoon black pepper

Remove the fibrous stems from the kale and discard. Rinse the greens in a colander and coarsely chop the leaves.

In a large, wide skillet, heat the oil and wine over medium heat. Add the mushrooms, onion, and garlic and cook, stirring, for 6 minutes. Stir in the kale and pepper and cook over medium heat, stirring frequently, until the greens are wilted, about 5 minutes.

Transfer the mixture to serving plates and serve.

Chapter 3

From Mild to Wild

Sauces, Dips, and Dressings

*T*he goals of a table condiment or sauce are to embellish, adorn, heighten, and enhance. Sometimes, a meal needs to be perked up or the palate craves a contrasting flavor or texture. This is the perfect time for a table sauce, such as a spicy salsa, tart chutney, or perhaps a bowl of pureed black beans. The main pillars of the vegan diet—pasta, rice, grains, and potatoes—are infinitely more interesting when paired with the proper sauce or topping. There is never a dull moment at the table when an appetizing sauce, dip, or dressing is part of the menu.

This chapter features a variety of enticing sauces, accompaniments, and dips. From Kiwi Vinaigrette, Black Bean Sofrito, and Marinara Magnifico to Jay's Tempting Salsa, Roasted Chili Hummus, and Papaya Guacamole, these condiments and sauces promise to electrify the palate and coax out the meal's optimal flavors. In addition, homemade sauces, dressings, and dips contributing negligible calories and fat are far healthier than traditional sauces or condiments such as hollandaise, mayonnaise, sour cream dips, or sugar-coated offerings stocked in grocery stores.

Whether spooned over the top, drizzled from above, or served on the side, these recipes promise a bounty of appealing tastes and pleasing textures. Whatever the occasion or mood, when in doubt, sauce it!

Kiwi Vinaigrette

Kiwifruits have a savory-sweet flavor and a soft texture and are loaded with vitamin C and other nutrients. Here, the small oval fruits are pureed into a delectable creamy dressing.

Yield: 2 cups (about 12 servings)

4	kiwifruits, peeled and coarsely chopped
¼	cup red wine vinegar or apple cider vinegar
¼	cup canola oil
1	tablespoon honey
½	teaspoon white pepper
¼	teaspoon salt

Place the kiwi, vinegar, oil, honey, pepper, and salt in a blender or food processor fitted with a steel blade. Process until smooth and creamy, 5 to 10 seconds.

Pour into a serving container and serve at once or refrigerate for later.

Helpful Tip:

For best results, use ripe, sweet kiwifruits. You can determine the ripeness by holding the kiwi in the palm of your hand and gently pressing down with your thumb; the fruit should give a little.

Classic Herb Vinaigrette

This versatile vinaigrette can be drizzled over tossed salads,
tossed with pasta, potatoes, or rice (in place of mayonnaise),
or lightly spooned over steamed vegetables.

Yield: About ⅔ cup (4 to 6 servings)

¼	cup plus 2 tablespoons canola oil
3	tablespoons red wine vinegar
1	tablespoon balsamic vinegar or rice vinegar
1½	teaspoons Dijon-style mustard
2	teaspoons honey
2	teaspoons mixture of dried herbs (oregano, basil, parsley, and thyme)
½	teaspoon black pepper
½	teaspoon salt
2	to 3 tablespoons chopped fresh herbs (such as basil, parsley, or mint)

Combine the oil, vinegars, mustard, honey, dried herb mixture, pepper, salt, and fresh herbs in a mixing bowl or jar and whisk thoroughly. Cover and refrigerate for 30 minutes to allow the flavors to meld.

Helpful Tip:

Make extra vinaigrette and store the leftover dressing in the refrigerator; it should keep for several weeks. The vinaigrette mellows as the flavors marinate and mingle. Whisk or shake well before serving.

Mango-Papaya Vinaigrette

This fruity dressing adds a taste of the tropics to the salad venue. The riper the fruit, the sweeter the dressing.

Yield: About 2 cups (12 to 14 servings)

1	large ripe mango, peeled, pitted, and diced
1	large papaya, peeled, seeded, and diced
⅓	cup canola oil
¼	cup apple cider vinegar
1	tablespoon honey
½	teaspoon white pepper
¼	teaspoon salt

Place the mango, papaya, oil, vinegar, honey, pepper, and salt in a food processor fitted with a steel blade or in a blender and process until smooth, 5 to 10 seconds.

Pour into a serving container. To serve, drizzle the dressing over tossed green salads. Refrigerate the remaining dressing for later.

Helpful Tip:

Mangoes and papayas are available in the produce section of well-stocked supermarkets and Latin American grocery stores.

Roasted Chili Hummus

Roasted chili peppers transform your basic hummus into an exciting dip or spread. Hummus also makes a tasty sandwich spread.

Yield: 2 cups

2	fresh New Mexico or poblano chili peppers
1	can (15 ounces) chick-peas
¼	cup tahini (sesame seed paste)
	Juice of 1 lemon
2	large cloves garlic, minced
¼	cup chopped fresh parsley
1	teaspoon ground cumin
½	teaspoon ground cayenne
½	teaspoon salt

Roast the chilies by placing them over an open flame or beneath an oven broiler until the outside skins are charred and puffy, 4 to 6 minutes. Remove the chilies from the heat and let cool for a few minutes. With a butter knife, scrape the charred skin from the flesh and discard. Remove the seeds and chop the flesh.

Drain the chick-peas, reserving about ¼ cup of the canned liquid. Add the roasted chilies, chick-peas and reserved liquid, tahini, lemon juice, garlic, parsley, cumin, cayenne, and salt to a food processor fitted with a steel blade or to a blender and process until smooth, about 10 seconds. Stop to scrape the sides with a spatula at least once.

Transfer the hummus to a serving bowl and serve with warm pita bread and/or raw vegetables.

Helpful Tip:

Look for tahini in Middle Eastern grocery stores or natural food stores.

Spicy Jalapeño–Black Bean Dip

A bowl of thick, pureed black beans is a wonderful sight. This dip is quick and simple to make and even easier to devour.

Yield: About 2 cups

1	can (15 ounces) black beans
1	tablespoon canola oil
1	small yellow onion, diced
1	medium tomato, diced
2	cloves garlic, minced
2	tablespoons chopped pickled jalapeños
2	whole scallions, trimmed and chopped
1½	teaspoons dried oregano
1	teaspoon ground cumin
½	teaspoon black pepper

Drain the beans, reserving ¼ cup of the liquid.

In a medium saucepan, heat the oil over medium heat. Add the onion, tomato, garlic, and jalapeños and cook, stirring, for 5 minutes. Add the beans and reserved liquid, scallions, oregano, cumin, and pepper and cook for about 7 minutes, stirring occasionally.

Transfer the mixture to a food processor fitted with a steel blade or to a blender and process until smooth, about 5 seconds. Pour the pureed mixture into a serving bowl.

Serve with warm flour tortillas, pita bread, or cut-up vegetables.

Garlicky Red Sauce

My Sicilian grandmother can prepare this delicious red sauce with her eyes shut. With a few cans of tomato paste, plenty of garlic, and a little basil and parsley, this masterful sauce is just minutes away.

Yield: 6 to 8 servings

2	tablespoons olive oil
4	cloves garlic, minced
4	cups water
2	cans (6 ounces each) tomato paste
2	teaspoons dried parsley
1	teaspoon dried basil
1	teaspoon sugar
½	teaspoon black pepper
½	teaspoon salt
1	pound cooked pasta

In a large saucepan, heat the oil over medium heat. Add the garlic and cook, stirring, until the garlic glistens, about 2 minutes. Add the water, tomato paste, parsley, basil, sugar, pepper, and salt and stir until a thick sauce is formed. Bring the sauce to a gradual simmer over medium-high heat, stirring frequently.

Reduce the heat to low and cook (partially covered) for 15 to 20 minutes, stirring occasionally. Remove the sauce from the heat and ladle over cooked pasta.

Marinara Magnifico

*This marinara sauce will satisfy the most ardent pasta lover.
The rich flavor of canned plum tomatoes is heightened with
herbs and slyly seasoned with garlic and onion.*

Yield: 2 cups (4 servings)

1	tablespoon olive oil
1	medium yellow onion, diced
2	large cloves garlic, minced
1	can (28 ounces) plum tomatoes
¼	cup chopped fresh parsley
1	teaspoon sugar (optional)
1	teaspoon dried oregano
1	teaspoon dried basil
½	teaspoon black pepper
½	teaspoon salt
½	pound cooked pasta

In a large saucepan, heat the oil over medium heat. Add the
onion and garlic and cook, stirring, for 4 minutes. Add the
tomatoes, parsley, optional sugar, oregano, basil, pepper, and
salt and bring to a simmer over medium-high heat. Reduce the
heat to low and cook for 20 minutes, stirring occasionally.

Transfer the sauce to a food processor fitted with a steel
blade or to a blender and process until smooth, about 5
seconds. Return the sauce to the pan and keep warm until
ready to serve over pasta.

Helpful Tip:

Canned plum tomatoes have a thick
and juicy flesh. They are available in
most well-stocked supermarkets.

Baba Ghanoush

This luscious Middle Eastern dip is made with roasted eggplant, garlic, tahini, and herbs. Serve it as a warm dip or sandwich spread.

Yield: About 1 ½ to 2 cups

2	medium eggplants, cut in half lengthwise
¼	cup tahini (sesame seed paste)
2	large cloves garlic, minced
3	to 4 tablespoons chopped fresh parsley
	Juice of 1 to 2 lemons
½	teaspoon ground cumin
½	teaspoon black pepper
½	teaspoon salt

Preheat the oven broiler.

Place the eggplant face down on a baking pan. Place beneath the broiler and roast until the skin crackles and the flesh is tender, about 10 minutes (flip the eggplant after about 8 minutes). Remove the pan from the oven and let cool slightly. Peel off the outer black skin from the eggplant and discard; coarsely chop the flesh.

In a medium mixing bowl, combine the tahini, garlic, parsley, lemon juice, cumin, pepper, and salt. Add the eggplant and mash the mixture with the back of a fork.

Transfer to a serving bowl and serve with pita bread or raw vegetables (or refrigerate for later—lasts up to 4 days).

Helpful Tip:
Look for tahini in Middle Eastern grocery stores or natural food stores.

Tropical
Barbecue Sauce

*Serve this fruity condiment with grilled vegetables, baked
potatoes, or roasted plantains.*

Yield: About 2 ½ cups

1	ripe mango, peeled, pitted, and diced
1	medium yellow onion, diced
1	medium carrot, diced
½	Scotch bonnet or 2 jalapeño chili peppers, seeded and minced
2	cloves garlic, minced
1	cup red wine vinegar
½	cup pineapple juice
2	tablespoons Worcestershire sauce
⅓	cup brown sugar
½	teaspoon salt
½	teaspoon ground allspice

In a large saucepan, combine the mango, onion, carrot, chili
pepper, garlic, vinegar, pineapple juice, Worcestershire sauce,
sugar, salt, and allspice and bring to a simmer over medium
heat. Reduce the heat to low and cook, stirring occasionally,
until the mixture has a jamlike consistency, 20 to 25 minutes.
Allow the mixture to cool to room temperature.

Place the mixture into a food processor fitted with a steel blade or in a blender and process until smooth, about 10 seconds.

Transfer the sauce to a serving bowl and serve warm or chilled. If refrigerated, the sauce should keep for several weeks.

Helpful Tip:

Fresh Scotch bonnet peppers are available in well-stocked supermarkets and Caribbean grocery stores.

Black Bean Sofrito

Sofrito is a versatile Puerto Rican table sauce traditionally served over soups, stews, and pilafs and other rice dishes. This variation includes earthy black beans and zesty cilantro.

Yield: 3 to 4 cups

1	tablespoon canola oil
1	medium yellow onion, diced
1	green bell pepper, seeded and diced
2	large cloves garlic, minced
1	can (15 ounces) black beans, drained
1	can (15 ounces) stewed tomatoes
½	teaspoon ground cumin
½	teaspoon black pepper
½	teaspoon salt
2	tablespoons chopped fresh cilantro

In a medium saucepan, heat the oil over medium-high heat. Add the onion, bell pepper, and garlic and cook, stirring, for 5 to 7 minutes. Add the beans, tomatoes, cumin, pepper, and salt and cook for 7 to 10 minutes over low heat, stirring frequently. Stir in the cilantro and remove from the heat.

Spoon the sofrito into a serving bowl and serve as a table sauce.

Green Tomato Chutney

Although green tomatoes are not as succulent as their red counterparts, the unripe mild fruits are welcome in sweet-and-tart chutneys and sauces. If your kitchen overflows with green tomatoes in autumn, this is a tasty way to use them. Chutney makes a healthful substitute for mayonnaise or butter in a variety of meals. Spoon it over baked potatoes or steamed vegetables, or toss it into a vegetable curry.

Yield: 4 cups (about 8 servings)

1	large yellow onion, diced
4	or 5 green tomatoes, diced
4	pears or apples, diced
1	cup red wine vinegar
1	cup apple cider
1	cup dark raisins
½	cup brown sugar
3	or 4 cloves garlic, minced
1	tablespoon minced fresh ginger root
1	teaspoon ground cumin
½	teaspoon black pepper
½	teaspoon salt
¼	teaspoon ground cloves

In a large saucepan, combine the onion, tomatoes, pears, vinegar, cider, raisins, sugar, garlic, ginger, cumin, pepper, salt, and cloves and bring to a simmer over medium heat. Reduce the heat to medium-low and cook for 45 minutes to 1 hour, stirring occasionally, until the mixture is chunky. Remove from the heat and let cool to room temperature.

Serve at once or refrigerate for later. If refrigerated, the chutney will keep for several weeks.

Mango-Pineapple Chutney

Mango chutney is a fruity, sweet-and-tart relish with roots in Indian cuisine. It makes a great low-fat topping for potatoes, curries, and cooked winter squash.

Yield: 4 cups (about 8 servings)

1	large mango, peeled, pitted, and diced
2	cups diced fresh pineapple
1	medium yellow onion, diced
1	large red apple, diced
1	cup red wine vinegar
½	cup apple juice
½	cup brown sugar
½	cup dark raisins
1	tablespoon minced fresh ginger root
3	or 4 cloves garlic, minced
½	teaspoon ground cumin
½	teaspoon ground cloves
¼	teaspoon salt

In a large saucepan, combine the mango, pineapple, onion, apple, vinegar, apple juice, sugar, raisins, ginger, garlic, cumin, cloves, and salt and bring to a simmer over medium heat. Reduce the heat to low and cook, stirring occasionally, until the mixture has a jam-like consistency, 20 to 30 minutes. Remove from the heat and let stand for 10 minutes.

Serve at once or refrigerate for later. If chilled, the chutney will keep for several weeks.

Autumn Cranberry Chutney

This sweet-and-sour condiment is a brilliant blend of cranberries, apples, vinegar, apple cider, and aromatic spices. Serve this versatile chutney with rice dishes, curries, scones, or grain pilafs.

Yield: About 2 ½ to 3 cups

1	package (12 ounces) fresh cranberries
2	red apples, diced
1	large yellow onion, diced
4	cloves garlic, minced
1	tablespoon minced fresh ginger root
¾	cup brown sugar
½	cup raisins
1½	cups red wine vinegar
1	cup apple cider
½	teaspoon black pepper
½	teaspoon ground cumin
½	teaspoon salt
¼	teaspoon ground cloves

In a large saucepan, combine the cranberries, apples, onion, garlic, ginger, sugar, raisins, vinegar, cider, pepper, cumin, salt, and cloves and bring to a simmer over medium heat. Reduce the heat to medium-low and cook, stirring occasionally, until the mixture has a jam-like consistency, 25 to 30 minutes. Allow the chutney to cool to room temperature.

Serve the chutney warm or refrigerate for later. If chilled, the chutney should keep for several weeks.

Sweet Pepper Rouille

Rouille is a Provençal-style sauce made with leftover bread. This dairy-free version can be served over pasta or rice or offered as a vegetable or cracker dip.

Yield: 3 cups (about 6 servings)

4	thick slices of French or Italian bread, crusts removed
1½	cups diced roasted red peppers (one 12-ounce jar)
2	tablespoons olive oil
2	cloves garlic, minced
½	teaspoon dried thyme
¼	teaspoon ground cayenne
¼	teaspoon salt
½	cup soy milk or rice milk
8	to 12 ounces cooked pasta
2	tablespoons chopped parsley

In a medium mixing bowl, soak the bread in warm water for about 5 seconds. Place the bread in a colander, drain, and gently squeeze out the excess water (like a sponge).

Transfer the soaked bread to a blender or food processor fitted with a steel blade. Add the roasted peppers, oil, garlic, thyme, cayenne, and salt. Process the mixture until smooth, about 5 seconds. Transfer the sauce to a medium saucepan and stir in the milk. Bring the sauce to a simmer over medium heat, stirring occasionally.

When ready, ladle the sauce over the cooked pasta and garnish with parsley.

Helpful Tip:

Roasted red peppers are available
in jars in the relish/pickle section of
grocery stores.

Salsa Verde

*Salsa verde (Spanish for "green sauce") is made with tart
tomatillos, cilantro, and hot peppers. Serve the sauce with
burritos, quesadillas, and other tortilla-based dishes.*

Yield: 1 ½ cups

1	tablespoon canola oil
1	small yellow onion, diced
2	cloves garlic, minced
1	can (12 ounces) whole tomatillos, drained
¾	cup vegetable stock
2	tablespoons pickled jalapeños, minced
½	teaspoon ground cumin
½	teaspoon black pepper
½	teaspoon salt
2	tablespoons chopped fresh cilantro

In a medium saucepan, heat the oil over medium-high heat.
Add the onion and garlic and cook, stirring, for 4 minutes. Add
the tomatillos, stock, jalapeños, cumin, pepper, and salt and
bring to a simmer over medium-high heat. Reduce the heat to
medium and cook for 7 minutes, stirring occasionally.

   Transfer the mixture to a blender or food processor fitted
with a steel blade and process until smooth, about 5 seconds.

Return to the pan and cook for about 10 minutes over medium-low heat, stirring occasionally. Stir in the cilantro.

Transfer the salsa to a bowl and serve with tortilla-based dishes (such as burritos) or as a dip. Refrigerate any leftover sauce for later.

Helpful Tip:

Canned tomatillos are available in the Mexican section of well-stocked supermarkets as well as Latin American grocery stores.

Jay's Tempting Salsa

This salsa is so tasty, you'll want to eat it by the spoonful. It is ideally served with burritos, quesadillas, or tortilla chips or as a topping for rice and beans, potatoes, or pilafs.

Yield: 4 cups

2	tomatoes, diced
1	green bell pepper, seeded and diced
1	medium yellow onion, diced
2	large cloves garlic, minced
1	to 2 jalapeño chili peppers, seeded and minced
2	tablespoons chopped fresh cilantro
	Juice of 1 lime
1	teaspoon ground cumin
1	teaspoon dried oregano
½	teaspoon black pepper
¼	teaspoon salt
¼	teaspoon ground cayenne
1	can (16 ounces) crushed tomatoes

In a large bowl, combine the tomatoes, bell pepper, onion, garlic, jalapeño, cilantro, lime juice, cumin, oregano, pepper, salt, cayenne, and crushed tomatoes and mix well. Place three quarters of the mixture in a food processor fitted with a steel blade and process for 5 seconds, creating a chunky vegetable mash.

Return the mash to the bowl and blend well. Chill the salsa for 30 minutes to 1 hour to allow the flavors to meld.

Piquant Creole Sauce

The "holy trinity" of Creole cooking—peppers, onions, and celery—form the basis of this prickly red sauce. Serve the sauce as a topping for pilafs or as a spicy sauce for pasta.

Yield: About 3 cups

1	tablespoon canola oil
1	green bell pepper, seeded and diced
1	medium yellow onion, diced
2	stalks celery, sliced
2	cloves garlic, minced
1	can (16 ounces) crushed tomatoes
½	cup water
2	teaspoons dried oregano
1½	teaspoons dried thyme
1	teaspoon Tabasco or other bottled hot sauce
½	teaspoon salt
½	teaspoon black pepper
¼	teaspoon white pepper
⅛	teaspoon ground cayenne

In a large saucepan, heat the oil over medium heat. Add the bell pepper, onion, celery, and garlic and cook, stirring, for 8 to 10 minutes. Add the tomatoes, water, oregano, thyme, Tabasco, salt, black and white pepper, and cayenne and bring to a simmer over medium-high heat. Reduce the heat to medium-low and cook for about 20 minutes, stirring occasionally. Remove from the heat.

Serve the sauce over rice or pasta. Refrigerate any leftovers for later.

Jay's Scotch Bonnet Nectar

As a chili pepper connoisseur, I like to collect an immense array of bottled hot sauces. Sometimes I take my passion one step further and prepare my own sauce. This fruity and fiery concoction is one of my favorites. Serve it as a condiment or barbecue sauce (and remember to warn your guests before serving!).

Yield: 2 cups

4	to 6 Scotch bonnet chili peppers, seeded and coarsely chopped
1	medium carrot, peeled and diced
1½	cups apple cider vinegar
1	ripe mango, peeled, pitted, and diced
½	cup diced red onion
	Juice of 1 lime
2	cloves garlic, minced
2	tablespoons brown sugar
¼	teaspoon ground turmeric

In a medium saucepan, combine the chili peppers, carrot, vinegar, mango, onion, lime juice, garlic, sugar, and turmeric and bring to a simmer over medium heat. Reduce the heat to medium-low and cook for 15 to 20 minutes, stirring occasionally.

Remove the sauce from the heat and let cool slightly. Ladle into a food processor fitted with a steel blade or into a blender and process until smooth, about 5 seconds. Transfer the sauce to a bowl and serve at once or refrigerate for later.

Helpful Tip:

Fresh Scotch bonnet peppers are available in well-stocked supermarkets and Caribbean grocery stores.

Papaya Guacamole

This marriage of papayas and avocados is a blissful union. If you like guacamole, you'll love this rendition. Serve it as a dip with tortilla chips or vegetables or as a condiment for burritos and other tortilla dishes.

Yield: 4 to 6 servings

2	ripe avocados, peeled, pitted, and chopped
1	papaya, peeled, seeded, and diced
1	large tomato, diced
¼	cup finely chopped red onion
2	cloves garlic, minced
2	tablespoons chopped fresh cilantro
	Juice of 1 lime
½	teaspoon ground cumin
½	teaspoon salt
½	teaspoon black pepper
2	whole scallions, trimmed and chopped

Place the avocados, papaya, tomato, onion, garlic, cilantro, lime juice, cumin, salt, and pepper into a food processor fitted with a steel blade or into a blender and process until chunky-smooth, about 5 seconds. (Or mash the ingredients in a mixing bowl with a large fork or spoon until a chunky paste is formed.)

Transfer the guacamole to a serving bowl and top with the scallions.

Helpful Tip:

For the best guacamole, use ripe avocados. You can determine an avocado's ripeness by holding it in the base of your hand and pressing down lightly with your thumb; it should give a little.

Thai Curry Sauce

Traditional Thai curries radiate with the exotic flavors of coconut milk, spicy curry paste, and aromatic herbs. Spoon this sauce over rice dishes, Asian noodles, steamed vegetables, or stir-fried meals.

Yield: 2 cups (about 8 servings)

1	tablespoon canola oil
1	small yellow onion, chopped
1	large clove garlic, minced
2	teaspoons Thai curry paste (preferably panang curry)
1	can (14 ounces) coconut milk
2	tablespoons light (low-sodium) soy sauce
	Juice of ½ lime
1	tablespoon cornstarch
1	tablespoon warm water
2	tablespoons chopped fresh cilantro or basil

In a medium saucepan, heat the oil over medium heat. Add the onion and garlic and cook, stirring, for 2 to 3 minutes. Stir in the curry paste and cook, stirring, for about 1 minute over low heat. Stir in the coconut milk, soy sauce, and lime juice and cook over medium-low heat until the mixture begins to simmer, about 5 minutes.

Meanwhile, in a small bowl, whisk the cornstarch with the warm water. While the curry sauce is simmering, gradually whisk in the cornstarch mixture and cook for 1 to 2 minutes, stirring frequently. The sauce should thicken slightly. Stir in the cilantro and remove from the heat.

Helpful Tip:

Look for Thai curry paste and coconut milk in Asian grocery stores and well-stocked supermarkets. Reduced-fat coconut milk should also be available.

Chapter 4

Lotsa Pasta!

*P*asta forms the foundation for a variety of delicious home-cooked meals. After all, who doesn't like pasta? This Italian import has become as American as apple pie and baseball. Scores of fancy-shaped pastas can be found in the aisles of supermarkets and natural food stores; gourmet pasta restaurants have opened up from coast to coast. Suddenly, pasta is everywhere.

Despite the dizzying shapes and sizes, traditional Italian dried pastas are processed from durum wheat flour (also called semolina). On the other side of the world, Asian noodles (such as lo mein and rice vermicelli) are made with rice flour, buckwheat flour, wheat flour, or in the case of cellophane noodles, mung beans. Furthermore, for those with adventurous palates, there is a cornucopia of gourmet noodles made from whole wheat flour, spinach, tomatoes, beets, quinoa, spelt, Jerusalem artichokes, and garlic and basil.

Cooking pasta is a breeze. The goal is to serve noodles that exhibit an "al dente" texture, meaning the texture is slightly firm, not too chewy nor soft. The routine is easy. In a large saucepan, bring plenty of water to a boil over medium-high heat (it is not necessary to add oil or salt). Place the pasta in the boiling water, stir the noodles, and quickly return to a gentle boil (slow-cooking the pasta over low heat results in sticky, floury noodles). Occasionally stir the pasta throughout the cooking process.

Always cook the pasta for the recommended cooking time. It is a good idea to check for doneness (al dente texture) about 1 to 2 minutes before the allotted time has elapsed. Do it the old-fashioned way: pull a noodle out of the water, cool it slightly, and bite into it. When the pasta is ready, pour the noodles into a colander and drain the cooking liquid. Do not run water over the pasta unless you are making pasta salad. Transfer the cooked pasta to warm serving plates and serve at once with your favorite sauce.

By itself, pasta is not fattening. However, when the noodles are drowned in a rich cream or butter sauce, the calorie meter starts to climb skyward. In the world of vegan cookery, pasta meals are both enticing and healthful. Canned and fresh tomatoes, seasonal vegetables, bountiful herbs, and aromatic garlic are the main staples, while soy sauce, cilantro, sesame oil, and peanut butter often appear in Asian recipes. The bottom line: If you stock your pantry with a variety of pastas, you will never get bored of this nourishing staple.

Hot Chili Macaroni

Macaroni, an all-American staple, blends nicely into this unpretentious one-pot dish of vegetable chili.

Yield: 6 servings

2	quarts water
1	cup elbow macaroni
1	tablespoon canola oil
1	medium yellow onion, diced
1	green bell pepper, seeded and diced
2	stalks celery, diced
3	or 4 cloves garlic, minced
1	can (28 ounces) stewed tomatoes
1	can (15 ounces) red kidney beans, drained
1	can (11 ounces) corn kernels, drained
1½	tablespoons chili powder
2	teaspoons dried oregano
1	teaspoon ground cumin
½	teaspoon black pepper
½	teaspoon salt

In a large saucepan, bring the water to a boil over medium-high heat. Add the macaroni, stir, and return to a boil. Cook over medium-high heat until al dente, about 6 minutes, stirring occasionally. Drain in a colander.

In a large saucepan, heat the oil over medium-high heat. Add the onion, bell pepper, celery, and garlic and cook, stirring, for 7 minutes. Stir in the tomatoes, beans, corn, chili powder, oregano, cumin, pepper, and salt and bring to a simmer. Cook over medium-low heat for 15 minutes, stirring occasionally. Blend in the cooked macaroni and cook for 5 minutes over low heat. Remove from the heat and let stand for 5 minutes before serving.

Ladle into bowls and serve at once.

Pasta Marinara with Broccoli

The secret to creating a great marinara sauce is to use canned plum tomatoes. They have a rich, robust flavor and thick texture. Broccoli adds a nice crunch to this dish.

Yield: 4 servings

1	tablespoon canola oil
1	medium yellow onion, diced
2	large cloves garlic, minced
1	can (28 ounces) plum tomatoes
2	tablespoons chopped fresh parsley
2	teaspoons dried oregano
1	teaspoon dried basil
½	teaspoon black pepper
½	teaspoon salt
3	quarts water
8	ounces pasta spirals or bow-tie pasta
1	small bunch broccoli, cut into florets
1	cup canned red kidney beans, drained

In a large saucepan, heat the oil over medium heat. Add the onion and garlic and cook, stirring, for about 4 minutes. Add the tomatoes, parsley, oregano, basil, pepper, and salt and bring to a simmer over medium-high heat. Reduce the heat to low and cook for 15 to 20 minutes, stirring occasionally.

In another large saucepan, bring the water to a boil over medium-high heat. Add the pasta, stir, and return to a boil. Cook for 8 minutes, then stir in the broccoli florets. Cook until the pasta is al dente, about 4 minutes, stirring occasionally. Drain the pasta and broccoli in a colander and transfer to a large serving dish.

Transfer the red sauce to a food processor fitted with a steel blade (or to a blender) and process until smooth, about 5 seconds. Return the sauce to the pan and stir in the beans. Return to a gentle simmer over medium heat.

Ladle the sauce over the pasta and broccoli and serve at once.

Spaghetti with Garden Greens

This is an easy way to include nutrient-rich leafy green vegetables into your everyday meals.

Yield: 4 servings

1	tablespoon canola oil
2	or 3 cloves garlic, minced
1	pound chard or field spinach, trimmed and cut into strips
¼	cup vegetable broth or water
½	teaspoon black pepper
½	teaspoon salt
3	quarts water
8	ounces spaghetti or linguine

In a large, wide skillet, heat the oil over medium heat. Add the garlic and cook, stirring, for 2 minutes. Add the chard, broth, pepper, and salt and cook, stirring, until the greens are wilted, 4 to 5 minutes.

In a large saucepan, bring the water to a boil over medium-high heat. Add the spaghetti, stir, and return to a boil. Cook over medium heat until al dente, 9 to 11 minutes, stirring occasionally. Drain in a colander.

Using tongs, transfer the pasta to a large serving bowl. Add the chard mixture and toss. Serve at once.

Spaghetti with Mushroom Marinara

A medley of mushrooms gives this rustic pasta dish an interesting, woodsy flavor.

Yield: 4 servings

2	tablespoons dry red wine
1	tablespoon olive oil
12	ounces white mushrooms, sliced
4	ounces cremini or shiitake mushrooms, sliced
1	small yellow onion, chopped
2	or 3 cloves garlic, minced
1	can (14 ounces) stewed tomatoes
1	can (14 ounces) tomato puree
2	teaspoons dried oregano
1	teaspoon dried basil
½	teaspoon dried red pepper flakes
½	teaspoon salt
2½	quarts water
8	ounces spaghetti

In a large saucepan, heat the wine and oil over medium heat. Add the mushrooms, onion, and garlic and cook, stirring, for 7 to 9 minutes. Stir in the tomatoes, tomato puree, oregano, basil, red pepper flakes, and salt. Reduce the heat to low and simmer for 15 to 20 minutes, stirring occasionally (partially cover the pan to prevent the sauce from splattering).

Meanwhile, in another large saucepan, bring the water to a boil over medium-high heat. Add the pasta, stir, and return to a boil. Cook over medium heat until al dente, 8 to 10 minutes, stirring occasionally. Drain in a colander.

When the sauce is ready, transfer the spaghetti to warm serving plates and spoon the sauce over the top.

Macaroni and Eggplant Ratatouille

Adding macaroni to ratatouille is a clever way to liven up this classic Mediterranean stew.

Yield: 6 servings

2½	quarts water
1	cup elbow macaroni
2	tablespoons dry red wine
1	tablespoon canola oil
1	medium yellow onion, diced
1	green bell pepper, seeded and diced
8	ounces white mushrooms, sliced
2	cups diced eggplant
3	or 4 cloves garlic, minced
1	can (28 ounces) plum or stewed tomatoes
1	can (15 ounces) red kidney beans, drained
2	teaspoons dried oregano
1	teaspoon dried basil
½	teaspoon black pepper
½	teaspoon salt

In a large saucepan, bring the water to a boil over medium-high heat. Add the macaroni, stir, and return to a boil. Cook over medium heat until al dente, about 6 minutes, stirring occasionally. Drain in a colander.

In another large saucepan, heat the wine and oil over medium heat. Add the onion, bell pepper, mushrooms, eggplant, and garlic and cook, stirring, for about 10 minutes. Stir in the tomatoes, beans, oregano, basil, pepper, and salt and bring to a simmer over medium-high heat. Reduce the heat to medium-low and cook for 15 minutes, stirring occasionally. (Cut the tomatoes into smaller pieces with the edge of a large spoon.)

Remove the ratatouille from the heat and fold in the cooked macaroni. Ladle into bowls and serve with warm Italian bread.

Penne with Swiss Chard

Tossing pasta with lemon-braised greens is an effortless way to jazz up a light pasta entree.

Yield: 4 servings

1	medium bunch red or green chard leaves
1	tablespoon olive oil
1	medium yellow onion, chopped
2	or 3 cloves garlic, minced
½	teaspoon black pepper
½	teaspoon salt
	Juice of 1 large lemon
2½	quarts water
8	ounces penne or ziti

Remove the fibrous stems of the chard leaves and discard. Rinse the leaves and cut into ribbon-shaped strips (chiffonade style).

In a large, wide skillet, heat the oil over medium heat. Add the onion and garlic and cook, stirring, for 3 minutes. Stir in the chard leaves, pepper, salt, and lemon juice. Cook until the greens are wilted and tender, about 5 minutes, stirring frequently. Set aside.

In a large saucepan, bring the water to a boil over medium-high heat. Add the pasta, stir, and return to a boil. Cook over medium heat until al dente, 8 to 10 minutes, stirring occasionally. Drain in a colander.

Add the pasta to the braised greens, toss, and serve at once.

Pasta with Oven-Broiled Vegetables

For this nutritious entree, linguine is tossed with broiled and lightly marinated vegetables. Meaty portobello mushrooms add a touch of panache.

Yield: 4 servings

1	tablespoon olive oil
2	tablespoons red wine vinegar
2	tablespoons chopped fresh parsley
1	teaspoon dried oregano
¼	teaspoon ground cayenne
½	teaspoon salt
1	zucchini, quartered lengthwise
1	medium red onion, quartered
1	red bell pepper, cored and seeded
3	or 4 portobello mushrooms, stems removed
2½	quarts water
8	ounces linguine or spaghetti

In a large bowl, combine the oil, vinegar, parsley, oregano, cayenne, and salt. Set aside.

Preheat the oven broiler.

Arrange the zucchini, onion, bell pepper, and mushrooms on a baking pan. Broil the vegetables until they are tender, about 5 minutes on each side. Remove the vegetables as they become done and transfer to a cutting board. Let cool slightly and then coarsely chop. Toss the vegetables with the dressing.

In a large saucepan, bring the water to a boil over medium-high heat. Add the pasta, stir, and return to a boil. Cook over medium heat until al dente, 8 to 10 minutes, stirring occasionally. Drain in a colander.

Add the pasta to the roasted vegetables and toss. Serve at once.

Pasta with Creole Ragu

The spicy, sturdy flavors of Creole cuisine are at center stage in this piquant noodle dish.

Yield: 6 servings

1	tablespoon canola oil
2	large carrots, chopped
1	medium yellow onion, diced
1	green bell pepper, seeded and diced
1	large celery stalk, diced
2	large cloves garlic, minced
1	can (28 ounces) stewed tomatoes
1	can (6 ounces) tomato paste
3	to 4 quarts plus ¾ cup water
1	tablespoon dried parsley
2	teaspoons dried oregano
½	teaspoon black pepper
½	teaspoon ground cayenne
2	to 3 teaspoons Tabasco or other bottled hot sauce
12	ounces linguine or spaghetti

In a large saucepan, heat the oil over medium heat. Add the carrots, onion, bell pepper, celery, and garlic and cook, stirring, until the vegetables are tender, about 7 minutes. Add the tomatoes, tomato paste, the ¾ cup of water, parsley, oregano, pepper, cayenne, and hot sauce and bring to a simmer over medium-high heat. Reduce the heat to medium-low and cook for about 15 minutes, stirring occasionally. As the sauce cooks, cut the chunks of tomatoes into smaller pieces with the edge of a large spoon.

Meanwhile, in a large saucepan, bring the 3 to 4 quarts of water to a boil over medium-high heat. Add the linguine, stir, and return to a boil. Cook over medium heat until al dente, 8 to 10 minutes, stirring occasionally. Drain in a colander.

Transfer the linguine to serving plates and ladle the sauce over the top. Serve at once.

Pasta with Garden Tomato Sauce

Zucchini, eggplant, and peppers give this fresh tomato sauce a robust taste and inviting texture.

Yield: 4 servings

1	tablespoon canola oil
1	medium zucchini, halved lengthwise and thinly cut diagonally
1	red or green bell pepper, seeded and cut into strips
2	cups diced eggplant
4	cloves garlic, minced
4	large tomatoes, diced
¼	cup chopped fresh basil or parsley
1	teaspoon dried oregano
1	teaspoon dried basil
1	teaspoon paprika
½	teaspoon black pepper
½	teaspoon salt
3	quarts water
8	ounces capellini or thin spaghetti

In a large skillet, heat the oil over medium-high heat. Add the zucchini, bell pepper, eggplant, and garlic and cook, stirring, for 7 to 9 minutes. Add the tomatoes, fresh basil, oregano, dried basil, paprika, pepper, and salt and cook for 10 minutes over medium heat, stirring occasionally. (As the tomatoes simmer, the mixture should thicken.)

Meanwhile, in a large saucepan, bring the water to a boil over medium-high heat. Add the pasta, stir, and return to a boil. Cook over medium heat until al dente, 7 to 9 minutes, stirring occasionally (if using capellini, cook 4 to 6 minutes). Drain the pasta in a colander.

Transfer the pasta to warm serving dishes and spoon the sauce over the top. Serve with warm bread.

Asian Vegetable Primavera

For this alluring entree, thin Asian noodles, stir-fried vegetables, and tofu are simmered in a soy- and ginger-scented broth.

Yield: 4 servings

3	quarts plus 1 tablespoon water
8	ounces rice noodles or buckwheat noodles
1	tablespoon peanut oil
1	red or yellow bell pepper, seeded and cut into strips
8	to 10 white mushrooms, sliced
6	fresh shiitake mushrooms, halved
2	teaspoons minced fresh ginger root
10	small leaves of bok choy or pat soi, cut into ribbons
4	whole scallions, trimmed and chopped
1	can (8 ounces) sliced water chestnuts, drained
¼	pound extra-firm tofu, cut into ¼-inch-wide matchsticks
½	cup vegetable broth
¼	cup low-sodium soy sauce
1	teaspoon sesame oil
1	tablespoon cornstarch
¼	cup unsalted roasted peanuts, chopped

In a large saucepan, bring the 3 quarts of water to a boil over medium-high heat. Add the noodles, stir, and cook over medium heat until al dente, 4 to 5 minutes, stirring occasionally. Drain in a colander.

In a large wok or skillet, heat the peanut oil over medium-high heat. Add the bell pepper, mushrooms, and ginger and stir-fry for 4 to 5 minutes. Stir in the bok choy, scallions, water chestnuts, and tofu and stir-fry for 4 minutes. Stir in the broth, soy sauce, and sesame oil and bring to a simmer over medium heat.

In a small mixing bowl, combine the cornstarch and the 1 tablespoon of water. Gradually drizzle the cornstarch mixture into the stir-fried mixture, stirring frequently. Return to a simmer over medium-high heat. Fold in the cooked noodles.

Spoon the vegetables and noodles onto warm plates. Sprinkle the peanuts over the top and serve at once.

Helpful Tip:

Shiitake mushrooms, water chestnuts, and bok choy can be found in Asian markets and well-stocked supermarkets.

Pasta with Country Ragu

Pasta and ragu go hand in hand. This country-style ragu is a chunky red sauce laden with carrots, tomatoes, and herbs.

Yield: 4 servings

1	tablespoon canola oil
2	large carrots, chopped
1	medium yellow onion, diced
1	large celery stalk, diced
2	large cloves garlic, minced
1	can (28 ounces) stewed tomatoes
3	tablespoons tomato paste
1	tablespoon dried parsley
2	teaspoons dried oregano
1	teaspoon dried basil
½	teaspoon black pepper
2½	quarts water
8	ounces linguine or spaghetti

In a large saucepan, heat the oil over medium heat. Add the carrots, onion, celery, and garlic and cook, stirring, until the vegetables are tender, 6 to 7 minutes. Add the tomatoes, tomato paste, parsley, oregano, basil, and pepper and bring to a simmer over medium-high heat. Reduce the heat to medium-low and cook for about 15 minutes, stirring occasionally. As the sauce cooks, cut the chunks of tomatoes into smaller pieces with the edge of a large spoon.

Meanwhile, in a large saucepan, bring the water to a boil over medium-high heat. Add the linguine, stir, and return to a boil. Cook over medium heat until al dente, 8 to 10 minutes, stirring occasionally. Drain in a colander.

Transfer the linguine to serving plates and ladle the sauce over the top.

Spaghetti Arrabiata

This spicy Italian meal with arrabiata sauce is seasoned with red pepper flakes, pickled pepperoncinis (light green Italian peppers), and fragrant herbs. The sauce smothers the pasta with a peppery, tomato flavor.

Yield: 4 servings

1	tablespoon olive oil
12	ounces white mushrooms, sliced
1	green bell pepper, seeded and cut into slivers (julienne style)
2	or 3 cloves garlic, minced
1	can (14 ounces) stewed tomatoes
1	can (14 ounces) tomato puree
2	or 3 pickled pepperoncinis, seeded and minced
2	teaspoons dried oregano
1	teaspoon dried basil
½	teaspoon dried red pepper flakes
½	teaspoon salt
3	quarts water
12	ounces spaghetti

In a large saucepan, heat the oil over high heat. Add the mushrooms, bell pepper, and garlic and cook over medium heat, stirring, for 7 to 9 minutes. Stir in the tomatoes, tomato puree, pepperoncinis, oregano, basil, red pepper flakes, and salt. Reduce the heat to medium-low and cook for 20 minutes, stirring occasionally.

Meanwhile, in another large saucepan, bring the water to a boil over medium-high heat. Add the pasta, stir, and return to a boil. Cook over medium heat until al dente, 8 to 10 minutes, stirring occasionally. Drain the spaghetti in a colander.

When the arrabiata sauce is ready, transfer the spaghetti to warm serving plates and spoon the sauce over the top. Serve with warm Italian bread.

Javanese Noodles with Lime-Peanut Sauce

Peanut butter, soy sauce, ginger, and lime are the central flavors in this Indonesian noodle dish.

Yield: 4 servings

1	tablespoon peanut oil
1	cup snow peas, coarsely chopped
1	tablespoon minced fresh ginger root
1	large jalapeño or serrano chili pepper, seeded and minced
½	pound extra-firm tofu, cut into ¼-inch-wide matchsticks
4	whole scallions, trimmed and chopped
½	cup roasted red peppers, diced
½	cup chunky peanut butter
¼	cup low-sodium soy sauce
1½	teaspoons sesame oil
	Juice of 1 large lime
2	to 3 tablespoons chopped cilantro
3	quarts water
8	ounces rice vermicelli

In a large wok or skillet, heat the peanut oil over medium-high heat. Add the snow peas, ginger, and jalapeño and stir-fry for 2 minutes. Stir in the tofu, scallions, and roasted peppers and stir-fry for 3 minutes. Reduce the heat to low; blend in the peanut butter, soy sauce, sesame oil, lime juice, and cilantro and cook for 2 minutes. Remove from the heat and let stand while the vermicelli cooks.

In a large saucepan, bring the water to a boil. Add the vermicelli, stir, and turn off the heat. Let the noodles steep in the water until al dente, about 5 minutes, stirring occasionally.

Drain the vermicelli in a colander and fold into the peanut sauce. Serve at once.

Helpful Tips:

Rice vermicelli can be found in Asian markets and well-stocked supermarkets. Roasted red peppers are available in jars in the relish/pickle section of grocery stores.

Gnocchi Eggplant Stew

Gnocchi is a dumpling-like pasta made from potatoes. The doughy, chewy "dumpling" is a favorite addition to one-pot stews and soups.

Yield: 4 servings

4	quarts water
12	ounces frozen gnocchi
2	tablespoons canola oil
1	medium yellow onion, diced
1	green bell pepper, seeded and diced
8	ounces white mushrooms, sliced
2	cups diced eggplant
4	cloves garlic, minced
1	can (15 ounces) crushed tomatoes
1	can (14 ounces) stewed tomatoes
1	tablespoon dried parsley
2	teaspoons dried oregano
½	teaspoon black pepper
½	teaspoon salt
¼	cup chopped fresh basil

In a large saucepan, bring the water to a boil over medium-high heat. Add the gnocchi, stir, and return to a boil. Cook over medium heat until al dente, about 5 minutes, stirring occasionally. Drain in a colander.

In another large saucepan, heat the oil over medium heat. Add the onion, bell pepper, mushrooms, eggplant, and garlic and cook, stirring, until the vegetables are tender, 8 to 10 minutes. Stir in the crushed tomatoes, stewed tomatoes, parsley, oregano, pepper, and salt and cook over medium-low heat for 15 minutes, stirring occasionally. Remove from the heat and stir in the cooked gnocchi and basil.

Ladle into bowls and serve with warm Italian bread.

Warm Thai Noodles with Soy Vinaigrette

For this quick-to-the-table dish, cellophane noodles are tossed with raw vegetables, soy sauce, ginger, and a hint of sugar. Cilantro adds a nice tangy flavor. Serve the noodles as a side dish or warm salad.

Yield: 4 servings

3	quarts water
4	ounces cellophane noodles
¼	pound extra-firm tofu, cut into ¼-inch-wide matchsticks
4	whole scallions, trimmed and chopped
4	radishes, thinly sliced
1	medium cucumber, peeled and diced
2	ounces mung bean sprouts
2	teaspoons minced fresh ginger root
¼	cup low-sodium soy sauce
1	tablespoon peanut oil
2	teaspoons brown sugar
1½	teaspoons toasted sesame oil
	Juice of 1 large lime
2	to 3 tablespoons chopped fresh cilantro

In a large saucepan, bring the water to a boil. Add the noodles, stir, and turn off the heat. Let the noodles soak until al dente, about 5 minutes, stirring occasionally. Drain in a colander and cool slightly under warm running water.

In a large mixing bowl, combine the tofu, scallions, radishes, cucumber, sprouts, ginger, soy sauce, peanut oil, sugar, sesame oil, lime juice, and cilantro and blend thoroughly. Toss the noodles into the bowl and blend again. Serve at once.

Stir-Fry Ginger Noodles with Tofu

For this vegetable and noodle dish, peanut butter thickens a soy sauce–based broth and adds a nutty dimension. The aroma of sesame oil and ginger are also present.

Yield: 4 servings

3	quarts water
8	ounces wide lo mein noodles
1	tablespoon peanut oil
1	red bell pepper, seeded and cut into thin strips
8	ounces white mushrooms, sliced
1	tablespoon minced fresh ginger root
2	cloves garlic, minced
10	to 12 broccoli florets
¼	pound extra-firm tofu, diced
½	cup vegetable broth
¼	cup soy sauce
1	tablespoon rice vinegar
1	tablespoon toasted sesame oil
1½	tablespoons peanut butter

In a large saucepan, bring the water to a boil over medium-high heat. Add the noodles, stir, and return to a boil. Cook until the noodles are al dente, about 5 minutes, stirring occasionally. Drain the noodles in a colander.

In a large skillet or wok, heat the peanut oil over medium-high heat. Add the bell pepper, mushrooms, ginger, and garlic and stir-fry for 5 minutes.

Stir in the broccoli and tofu and stir-fry for 3 to 4 minutes. Stir in the broth, soy sauce, rice vinegar, and sesame oil and bring to a simmer. Cook, stirring, for 4 minutes. Reduce the heat to low and blend in the peanut butter. Fold in the lo mein noodles.

Transfer the mixture to serving plates and serve at once.

Middle Eastern Noodle Pilaf

Noodles and rice meld nicely together in this savory pilaf. To create a "toasty" nuance, thin noodles are roasted in a skillet and then combined in the pot with brown rice and the remaining ingredients.

Yield: 4 servings

6	ounces capellini, vermicelli, or angel hair pasta
1	tablespoon canola oil
1	tablespoon olive oil
1	medium yellow onion, diced
1	red bell pepper, seeded and diced
3½	cups vegetable broth or water
1¼	cups long-grain brown rice
2	medium carrots, diced
½	teaspoon ground turmeric
½	teaspoon black pepper
½	teaspoon ground cumin
½	teaspoon salt
1	can (15 ounces) chick-peas, drained

Break the capellini into small pieces (this can be done over a large bowl with your hands).

In a large skillet, heat the canola oil over medium heat. Add the capellini and cook, stirring, until the noodles are golden brown, about 5 minutes. Remove the pan from the heat.

In another large saucepan, heat the olive oil over medium heat. Add the onion and bell pepper and cook, stirring, for 4 to 5 minutes. Stir in the broth, rice, carrots, turmeric, pepper, cumin, and salt and bring to a simmer over high heat. Stir the grains, cover the pan, and cook over low heat for 10 minutes. Stir in the roasted capellini and chick-peas, cover, and cook until all of the liquid is absorbed, 20 to 25 minutes (stir the pot after about 10 minutes).

Remove the pilaf from the heat and fluff the grains and noodles. Let stand for 5 to 10 minutes before serving.

Ziti with Exotic Mushrooms

The growing availability of fancy mushrooms is a boon to the adventurous cook. For this dish, a medley of mushrooms enlivens a delicious red sauce for ziti.

Yield: 4 servings

2	tablespoons olive oil
8	ounces white mushrooms, sliced
6	ounces fresh cremini mushrooms, sliced
4	ounces fresh oyster or shiitake mushrooms, sliced
4	cloves garlic, minced
1	can (14 ounces) stewed tomatoes
1	can (14 ounces) tomato puree
3	quarts plus ¼ cup water
2	teaspoons dried oregano
1	teaspoon dried basil
½	teaspoon black pepper
½	teaspoon salt
¼	cup coarsely chopped fresh basil
12	ounces ziti or penne

In a large saucepan, heat the oil over medium heat. Add the mushrooms and garlic and cook, stirring, for 7 to 8 minutes. Stir in the tomatoes, tomato puree, the ¼ cup of water, oregano, dried basil, pepper, and salt. Reduce the heat to low and simmer for 20 minutes, stirring occasionally. Stir in the fresh basil and remove from the heat.

Meanwhile, in a large saucepan, bring the 3 quarts of water to a boil. Add the pasta, stir, and return to a boil. Cook over medium heat until al dente, about 10 minutes, stirring occasionally. Drain the pasta in a colander and transfer to warm plates.

Spoon the sauce over the pasta and serve with Italian bread.

Helpful Tip:

Look for fresh cremini, oyster, and shiitake mushrooms in the produce section of well-stocked grocery stores and specialty markets.

Rigatoni with Ratatouille Red Sauce

Large, tube-shaped rigatoni is best matched with a thick, robust sauce. This hearty ratatouille-style sauce with black beans aptly fills the bill.

Yield: 3 to 4 servings

2	tablespoons dry red wine
1	tablespoon olive oil
1	medium yellow onion, diced
2	cups diced eggplant
1	small zucchini, diced
2	cloves garlic, minced
1	can (28 ounces) plum tomatoes
1	can (15 ounces) black beans, drained
2	teaspoons dried oregano
2	teaspoons dried basil
½	teaspoon salt
¼	teaspoon dried red pepper flakes
3	quarts water
8	ounces rigatoni

In a large saucepan, heat the wine and oil over medium-high heat. Add the onion, eggplant, zucchini, and garlic and cook, stirring, for about 8 minutes. Add the tomatoes, beans, oregano, basil, salt, and red pepper flakes and bring to a simmer. Reduce the heat to medium-low and cook for 15 minutes, stirring occasionally. With the edge of a large spoon, cut the large chunks of tomatoes into smaller pieces.

Meanwhile, in a large saucepan, bring the water to a boil over medium-high heat. Add the rigatoni, stir, and return to a boil. Cook over medium heat until al dente, about 14 minutes, stirring occasionally. Drain the pasta in a colander.

Place the rigatoni in a large bowl and ladle the sauce over the top. Serve at once.

Chapter 5

Vegan Pantry Staples
Rice, Grains, and Legumes

Rice, grains, and beans are the essential building blocks of the healthful vegan diet. With a wide selection of rices, grains, and legumes in your kitchen, there will always be a variety of meal choices to whet your appetite. In addition, this versatile trio of staples is an excellent source of complex carbohydrates, fiber, plant proteins, and antioxidants.

All About Rice

Rice is considered to be one of the world's most versatile grains. From pilaf, paella, and jambalaya to risotto, burrito, and rice pudding, there are a plethora of enticing rice-inspired dishes. What's more, there is a smorgasbord of varieties to choose from. Basmati, jasmine, Wehani, wild rice, arborio, and venerable brown rice are just some of the kinds of rice available in natural food stores and supermarkets. Rice is highly nutritious, easy to digest, and economical.

All rices are not created equal. Brown rice is chewier, nuttier, and a better source of fiber and essential nutrients than is white rice. On the other hand, white rice tends to be fluffier, lighter, faster-cooking, and less expensive. Although white rice has been stripped of its nutrient-dense bran during the milling process, it is later enriched with niacin, thiamin, and iron. However, most of the dietary fiber and other important nutrients are lost.

Still, there is a place in the kitchen for exotic white rices such as arborio, basmati, jasmine, and Wild Pecan. When serving white rice, it is important to include plenty of nutrient-dense ingredients in the dish. Adding beans, lentils, tofu, cruciferous vegetables (such as broccoli or kale), winter squash, and/or leafy greens will bring lively flavors as well as valuable nutrients to the meal. Mixing whole grains or brown rice with white rice is another way to increase the overall nutrient value while satisfying the appetite.

A Glossary of Rices

Here is a guide to the multitude of rices that can be found in well-stocked supermarkets, natural food stores, and ethnic pantries.

Arborio is a short, pearly white grain used to make Italian risotto. Cooked arborio rice turns soft and creamy, not fluffy like most American rices. Arborio can be used in soups, rice puddings, and scores of variations of risotto. Unlike other rices, arborio should be stirred while it cooks.

Basmati is an aromatic, nutty rice grown in India and Pakistan (basmati means "queen of fragrance"). The cooked grains become slender, tender, and fluffy. Both brown basmati and white basmati are available. Another variety, kasmati, is a basmati-style rice grown in the United States.

Black japonica is a blackish-purple rice grown in Southeast Asia and California. Black japonica has a mild nutty flavor and soft texture. The grain is often combined with other whole grain rices and marketed as a gourmet rice blend.

Brown rice is a beige grain with a nutty flavor and chewy texture. Brown rice has its nutrient-dense bran layer still intact and contains twice the fiber as polished white rice. Brown rice takes about 30 to 40 minutes to cook. Varieties include short, medium, and long grains.

Jasmine rice has a fragrant, popcorn-like aroma and nutty flavor similar to basmati. The tender grains become moist and sticky when cooked. Native to Thailand, jasmine is also called Thai Fragrant. Jasmine only takes 12 to 15 minutes to cook. A similar rice, called jasmati, is grown in the United States.

Parboiled rice, also called "converted" rice (Uncle Ben's trademark), was invented to meet the American penchant for fluffy rice. The harvested rice is soaked in water, pressurized and steamed, and then dried. The resulting "parboiled rice" remains separate when cooked. The rice takes slightly longer to cook than regular white rice and requires slightly more liquid. (Parboiled rice should not be confused with instant rice, a product that is completely precooked and devoid of most nutrients, texture, and flavor.)

Wehani is a mahogany-colored whole grain rice marketed by Lundberg Family Farms in California. The rice has a rustic, nutty flavor and a texture similar to brown rice. Wehani can be added to pilafs, salads, and one-pot rice dishes.

White long-grain rice is one of the most common grains in the world. To create polished white rice, the outer bran layers are removed in the milling process. In the process, fiber and essential nutrients are lost. American rice is later enriched with thiamin, niacin, and riboflavin—but many of the nutrients and fiber cannot be replaced. When cooking with white rice, it is important to add a variety of nutrient-dense staples to the dish, such as beans, lentils, sturdy vegetables, leafy greens, squash, and tofu.

Whole grain rice blends refers to a variety of gourmet rice mixtures available in the marketplace. The gourmet blends often include brown rice, wild rice, black japonica rice, and mahogany-hued rices. Whole grain rice blends are interchangeable with brown rice in most recipes.

Wild rice is not really a rice, but a dark seed of a native North American aquatic grass. The grain has a firm and chewy texture and distinctive grassy flavor and aroma. Wild rice is harvested in the northern lakes in Minnesota and Canada (and is quite expensive). Wild rice takes about 45 to 50 minutes to cook, and 1 cup requires at least 3 cups of cooking liquid. The grain is best appreciated by blending with other whole grains.

All About Grains

Whole grains are growing in availability and are excellent sources of complex carbohydrates, plant protein, vitamins, iron, and dietary fiber. Whole grains readily absorb other flavors in the pot and add chewy textures and substance—without the fat.

Grains are easy to cook, but the cooking times will vary significantly depending on the variety. Couscous and bulgur cook up in minutes by steeping in hot water. Quinoa, millet, and amaranth cook as fast as white rice. Barley requires 45 minutes or longer to cook—but the wait is worth it!

A Glossary of Grains

Here is a guide to the wide selection of super grains found in well-stocked supermarkets, natural food stores, and ethnic pantries.

Amaranth are beige grains shaped like poppy seeds. The ancient grains have a nutty flavor and creamy, porridge-like texture and take about 25 minutes to cook. (Amaranth also refers to the plant's leafy greens, which are marked with streaks of red. Amaranth greens are cooked like a leafy green vegetable.)

Barley is a kernel-shaped, mild grain with comfort-food appeal. Although most of the barley in this country is processed into malt for beer consumption, the earthy grains lend chewy substance to stews, soups, salads, and pilafs. Barley blends well with woodsy mushrooms and sturdy vegetables for an easy pilaf or wintry soup. Barley is often sold in the "pearled" form (which has been hulled or milled). It takes about 40 to 45 minutes to cook. Barley is a great source of cholesterol-lowering soluble fiber.

Bulgur refers to whole wheat berries that have been precooked, dried, cracked, and sifted. The grain is famous for inspiring tabbouleh, the Middle Eastern wheat-and-vegetable salad. To cook bulgur, simply steep the grains in boiling water for 15 to 30 minutes and drain off the excess liquid. The grains can be fluffed into multigrain salads, bean dishes, and chilled soups such as gazpacho. (Do not confuse bulgur with cracked wheat, a grain that has not been precooked and requires a slightly longer cooking time.)

Corn seems closer to a vegetable than a grain, but when it is dried and ground, **cornmeal** (the grain) is born. Cornmeal forms the basis of hearty accompaniments such as corn bread, polenta, corn muffins, tortillas, johnnycakes, and pancakes. Corn bread makes a savory accompaniment to spicy chili, gumbo, jambalaya, and black bean soup. Traditional corn bread tends to be rather dry, but adding corn kernels, cheese, or chipotle peppers is a way to improve the moistness and flavor.

Couscous is not technically a grain but a tiny grain-like pasta made from fine semolina, the wheat flour used for spaghetti and other pastas. The grains take only 10 minutes to cook (by steeping in hot water). As a salad ingredient, couscous combines well with a delicate dressing such as lemon or lime vinaigrette, herbs, and legumes. For more fiber, try whole wheat couscous.

Quinoa (pronounced "keen-wa") is an ancient beige grain that has been grown in the rugged highlands of South America for centuries. The small, ring-like grains have a nutty flavor and moist, dense texture. Quinoa can be combined with (or substituted for) rice in pilafs, soups, salads, and side dishes. The versatile "mother grain" cooks in only 15 to 20 minutes—just as fast as rice. Remember to rinse uncooked quinoa thoroughly to wash away the natural, bitter-tasting resin (saponin) that coats the grains. Quinoa is one of the best sources of plant proteins.

Spelt sounds like a fad-of-the-month grain, but like amaranth and quinoa, it has been cultivated for centuries. Spelt is a lesser-known cousin of wheat and is processed into baking flour, cereals, and an assortment of pastas. Spelt pasta has a dark color and grainy flavor and cooks just like regular semolina pasta.

All About Legumes

Legumes include the diverse family of dried beans, split peas, and lentils. Legumes are good sources of dietary fiber, protein, iron, calcium, and complex carbohydrates. In addition, legumes are naturally low in fat, calories, and sodium. Versatile and economical, legumes add substance, texture, and flavors to almost any meal, from hearty soups, salads, and grain dishes to breakfast fare and vegetable dips. Legumes also take a long time to digest and provide a full, satisfied feeling after a meal.

A Glossary of Legumes

Legumes come in multiple shapes, sizes, and colors. Here is a description of some popular legumes that can be found in the healthy pantry.

Adzuki beans, also called azuki beans, are small, burgundy-red beans with a nutty, slightly sweet flavor. Popular in Asian cuisine, adzuki beans are often combined with rice for a dish called red rice. Adzuki are also cooked, mashed, and sweetened and used as a filling for Asian pastries, breads, and turnovers.

Anasazi beans are ancient heirloom beans grown in Colorado and the American Southwest. Anasazi beans have a slight kidney shape and reddish-purple skin with creamy mottled streaks. The beans can be added to chili, soups, and hearty stews.

Black beans are oval, pea-shaped beans with an earthy, woodsy flavor. Popular in Latin American, Caribbean, and Mexican cuisine, black beans inspire hearty soups, salads, dips, chilies, and rice dishes. Brazilian feijoada, Cuban beans and rice, and Mexican black bean soup (sopa feijoa negro) are some classic black bean dishes.

Black-eyed peas are round, creamy white beans with a distinctive dark "eye" on its ridges. They have an earthy, mealy flavor and firm texture. Black-eyed peas are prevalent in the American South, Africa, the Caribbean, and the Middle East. The Southern dish called Hoppin' John is made with black-eyed peas.

Chick-peas, also called garbanzo beans or ceci beans, are shaped like tiny tan-colored acorns. Popular in Mediterranean, Indian, Caribbean, and Middle Eastern cooking, chick-peas have a chewy texture and nutty nuance. The versatile beans are used in hummus, pasta dishes, vegetable soups, pilafs, and multibean salads.

Cranberry beans, also called Roman beans, are oval beans with a speckled, beige-and-cranberry skin. Similar to pinto beans in flavor, cranberry beans are common in Italian, Native American, and South American stews and soups.

Lentils come in brown, green, red, orange, black, and yellow colors. The elliptical, disc-shaped lentils cook faster than most legumes and are also easy to digest. Lentils are a mainstay of Indian, Middle Eastern, North African, and European cooking and are commonly used in Indian dal, vegetable curries, hearty soups, and grain salads.

Pigeon peas, also called gungo peas, are small, pea-shaped tannish-yellow beans with a tiny eye and faint freckle marks. The pea-shaped beans are a favored legume in Caribbean soups, stews, and grain dishes such as peas and rice.

Pinto beans are mottled, pinkish-brown beans with a mealy bean flavor. When cooked, the pinto markings (named after the horse) fade to pink. Pintos are a staple of Mexican, Tex-Mex, Southwestern, and Native American fare (refried beans are made with pinto beans).

Red kidney beans are, as their name implies, kidney-shaped beans with a rich, meaty flavor and chewy texture. Common varieties include dark red, light red, and white beans. Kidney beans are used Latin American, Caribbean, and Creole/Cajun cooking and inspire robust chilies, soups, bean-and-rice salads, three-bean salads, vegetable stews, and countless varieties of pilafs.

Soybeans, also called soya beans, are about the size of large peas. Tannish-yellow soybeans are available in America, but Asian varieties include black, green, brown, and red versions. Soybeans are often processed into a variety of soy foods, such as soy sauce, tamari, miso, soy milk, soy flour, tofu, tempeh, fermented bean pastes, and soybean oil. Soybeans require a long cooking time—several hours, in fact.

Split peas are whole green or yellow peas that have been split in half. Well-cooked split peas develop a porridge-like consistency and wholesome grassy flavor. Split peas are prevalent in Mediterranean, European, Indian, and traditional American meals and are famous for inspiring myriad versions of soothing split pea soup.

White beans refers to a collection of legumes, which include Great Northern, white kidney beans (cannellini beans), and small, oval navy beans. White beans are prevalent in European cuisines and are used in casseroles, soups, and stews. Boston baked beans and senate bean soup are both prepared with white beans.

Asparagus Pilaf with Artichokes

Two enticing vegetables, asparagus and artichokes, team up in this nourishing pilaf.

Yield: 4 servings

1	tablespoon canola oil
1	medium yellow onion, diced
8	to 10 white mushrooms, chopped
2	large cloves garlic, minced
1½	cups long-grain white rice
3½	cups water or vegetable broth
1	can (14 ounces) artichoke hearts, rinsed and coarsely chopped
10	to 12 asparagus spears, trimmed and cut into 1-inch pieces
¼	cup chopped fresh parsley
1½	teaspoons curry powder
½	teaspoon black pepper
½	teaspoon salt
	Juice of 1 or 2 lemons (optional)

In a medium saucepan, heat the oil over high heat. Add the onion, mushrooms, and garlic, and cook, stirring, for about 5 minutes. Stir in the rice, water, artichokes, asparagus, parsley, curry powder, pepper, and salt and bring to a simmer over medium-high heat. Stir the grains, cover, and cook over medium-low heat until the rice is tender, 15 to 20 minutes.

Fluff the rice and let stand for 5 to 10 minutes before serving. If desired, squeeze the lemon juice over the pilaf.

Multigrain Vegetable Pilaf

A trio of grains forms a delectable alliance in this savory one-pot dish.

Yield: 4 servings

1	tablespoon canola oil
8	to 10 white mushrooms, chopped
2	medium carrots, diced
1	medium yellow onion, chopped
1	green or red bell pepper, seeded and diced
2	or 3 cloves garlic, minced
3	cups vegetable broth or water
1	cup brown rice or brown basmati rice
¼	cup wild rice
1	teaspoon curry powder
½	teaspoon black pepper
½	teaspoon salt
½	cup couscous
½	cup boiling water

In a large saucepan, heat the oil over medium heat. Add the mushrooms, carrots, onion, bell pepper, and garlic and cook, stirring, for 6 to 7 minutes. Add the broth, both rices, curry powder, pepper, and salt. Stir the grains and bring to a simmer over medium-high heat. Cover and cook over low heat until the grains are tender, 40 to 45 minutes.

Meanwhile, in a small bowl, combine the couscous and boiling water. Stir the grains, cover, and set aside for about 15 minutes.

When the pilaf is done, fluff the grains and fold in the couscous. Let stand for 5 minutes before serving.

Orzo and Sweet Pea Pilaf

Orzo is an oval, rice-shaped pasta with a soft texture. It is often blended with rice in pilafs and one-pot dishes.

Yield: 4 servings

1	tablespoon olive oil
1	medium yellow onion, chopped
2	or 3 cloves garlic, minced
1	cup long-grain white rice
½	cup orzo
½	teaspoon salt
½	teaspoon black pepper
¼	teaspoon ground turmeric
2¾	cups water
1	cup green peas, fresh or frozen
¼	cup chopped pimientos or roasted red peppers
2	tablespoons chopped fresh parsley

In a medium saucepan, heat the oil over medium heat. Add the onion and garlic and cook, stirring, for 4 minutes. Stir in the rice, orzo, salt, pepper, and turmeric and cook for 1 minute over low heat, stirring frequently. Add the water, green peas, and pimientos and bring to a simmer over medium-high heat. Stir the grains, cover, and cook over low heat until the grains are tender, 15 to 20 minutes.

Remove from the heat, fluff the grains, and blend in the parsley. Let stand for 5 to 10 minutes before serving.

Helpful Tip:

Orzo, also called rosa maria, is available in the pasta section of most grocery stores.

Lemony Artichoke Pilaf

Lemon and artichokes complement each other in this tangy rice dish.

Yield: 4 servings

1	tablespoon olive oil
1	medium yellow onion, diced
1	red bell pepper, seeded and diced
1	small zucchini, diced
2	cloves garlic, minced
1½	cups long-grain white rice
3	cups water
1	can (14 ounces) artichoke hearts, rinsed and coarsely chopped
¼	cup chopped fresh parsley
½	teaspoon black pepper
½	teaspoon salt
4	whole scallions, trimmed and chopped
	Juice of 2 lemons

In a large saucepan, heat the oil over medium heat. Add the onion, bell pepper, zucchini, and garlic and cook, stirring, for about 6 minutes. Stir in the rice, water, artichokes, parsley, pepper, and salt and bring to a simmer over medium-high heat. Stir the grains, cover, and cook over low heat until the rice is tender, 15 to 20 minutes.

Fluff the rice and blend in the scallions and lemon juice. Let stand for 5 to 10 minutes before serving.

Yellow Spice Rice

This curry-scented dish is enriched with chick-peas, onions, and garlic. Versatile and easy to prepare, the side dish is appropriate for almost any occasion.

Yield: 4 servings

1	tablespoon canola oil
1	medium red onion, diced
1	red bell pepper, seeded and diced
2	cloves garlic, minced
1½	teaspoons curry powder
1	teaspoon ground cumin
¼	teaspoon ground turmeric
½	teaspoon salt
½	teaspoon black pepper
1½	cups long-grain white rice or basmati rice
3	cups water
1	can (15 ounces) chick-peas, drained
¼	cup chopped fresh parsley

In a medium saucepan, heat the oil over medium heat. Add the onion, bell pepper, and garlic and cook, stirring, for about 5 minutes. Add the curry powder, cumin, turmeric, salt, and pepper and cook, stirring, for 30 seconds. Stir in the rice and water and bring to a simmer over medium-high heat. Reduce the heat to medium-low, stir in the chick-peas, and cover. Cook until the rice is tender, 15 to 20 minutes.

Remove from the heat, fluff the rice, and fold in the parsley. Let stand for 5 to 10 minutes before serving.

Jollof Vegetable Rice

This festive "party dish" is rooted in West African cuisine. Curry, ginger, and thyme underscore the dish with pungent, aromatic flavors.

Yield: 4 servings

1	tablespoon canola oil
1	medium yellow onion, chopped
1	green bell pepper, seeded and diced
2	teaspoons minced fresh ginger root
2	large tomatoes, diced
2	to 3 teaspoons curry powder
2	teaspoons dried thyme leaves
½	teaspoon black pepper
½	teaspoon salt
1½	cups long-grain white rice
3	cups water
2	cups chopped fresh leafy greens (such as spinach, collard, or kale)
2	large carrots, diced
1	tablespoon tomato paste
1	can (15 ounces) black-eyed peas, drained

In a large saucepan, heat the oil over medium-high heat. Add the onion, bell pepper, and ginger and cook, stirring, for 5 to 7 minutes. Add the tomatoes, curry powder, thyme, pepper, and salt and cook, stirring, for about 2 minutes. Stir in the rice, water, greens, carrots, and tomato paste and bring to a simmer over medium-high heat. Stir the grains, cover, and cook over low heat until most of the liquid is absorbed, about 15 minutes.

Fluff the rice, stir in the black-eyed peas, recover, and cook for 5 minutes more. Let stand (still covered) for about 10 minutes before serving.

Green Lentil and Bulgur Stew

When cooked together, lentils and bulgur are a nutritious duo. They are often paired into a simple, family-style meal, as in this Middle Eastern dish.

Yield: 3 to 4 servings

1	cup dried green lentils, rinsed
4½	cups water
½	cup coarse bulgur
½	teaspoon salt
½	teaspoon black pepper
1	to 2 tablespoons olive oil
1	medium yellow onion, slivered

In a large saucepan, combine the lentils and water and bring to a simmer over medium-high heat. Reduce the heat to medium and cook for about 25 minutes, stirring occasionally. Add the bulgur, salt, and pepper and cook until the lentils are tender, 15 to 20 minutes, stirring occasionally. (Add a little hot water if necessary.)

In a large skillet, heat the oil over medium-high heat. Add the onion and cook, stirring, until the onion slivers are browned, 7 to 10 minutes. Stir the onions into the pot of lentils and bulgur.

Serve the grains with pita bread and a tossed green salad.

Three-Vegetable Bulgur Pilaf

This grain-and-vegetable entree is enhanced with fresh lemon at the finish.

Yield: 4 servings

1½	cups coarse bulgur
3	cups water
½	cup chopped fresh parsley
1	teaspoon ground cumin
1	teaspoon ground coriander
½	teaspoon black pepper
½	teaspoon salt
1½	tablespoons olive oil
1	medium yellow onion, diced
1	green or red bell pepper, seeded and cut into strips
1	medium yellow zucchini, diced
2	whole scallions, trimmed and chopped
1	large lemon, quartered

In a medium saucepan, combine the bulgur, water, parsley, cumin, coriander, pepper, and salt and bring to a simmer over medium-high heat. Remove from the heat and stir the grains. Let stand until the bulgur has absorbed all of the water, about 15 minutes.

In a large saucepan, heat the oil over medium heat. Add the onion, bell pepper, and zucchini and cook, stirring, for about 7 minutes. Stir in the cooked bulgur and scallions and cook for 2 to 3 minutes over medium heat, stirring occasionally.

Squeeze the lemon over the pilaf and serve at once.

Pumpkin, Corn, and Bean Stew

For centuries the "three sisters" of the garden—pumpkin, corn, and beans—have been grown together in America. They make natural companions in this rustic stew-meal.

Yield: 4 servings

1	tablespoon canola oil
1	medium yellow onion, diced
2	or 3 cloves garlic, minced
1	large jalapeño chili pepper, seeded and minced
2	large tomatoes, diced
1	tablespoon paprika
1	tablespoon dried oregano
1	tablespoon dried parsley
1	teaspoon ground cumin
½	teaspoon salt
4	cups peeled, diced pumpkin or butternut squash
2	cups water
2	cups corn kernels, fresh or frozen
1	can (15 ounces) cranberry beans or red kidney beans, drained

In a large saucepan, heat the oil over medium heat. Add the onion, garlic, and jalapeño and cook, stirring, for about 5 minutes. Add the tomatoes, paprika, oregano, parsley, cumin, and salt and cook, stirring, for 3 to 4 minutes. Add the pumpkin and water and bring to a simmer over medium-high heat. Reduce the heat to medium-low and cook until the pumpkin is tender, about 25 minutes, stirring occasionally. Stir in the corn and beans and cook for about 10 minutes. To thicken, mash the pumpkin with a large spoon against the side of the pan.

Serve the stew over a bed of quinoa or rice.

Green Split Pea and Barley Stew

Split peas and barley unite to form a "stick to your ribs" stew—perfect for a cold winter day or lazy afternoon.

Yield: 6 servings

1	tablespoon canola oil
1	medium yellow onion, diced
2	stalks celery, diced
2	large carrots, diced
3	or 4 cloves garlic, minced
6	cups water
1	cup green split peas, rinsed
½	cup pearl barley
2	large white potatoes, coarsely chopped
2	tablespoons dried parsley
2	teaspoons dried oregano or thyme leaves
½	teaspoon black pepper
2	cups chopped fresh spinach
	About 1 teaspoon salt

In a large saucepan, heat the oil over medium heat. Add the onion, celery, carrots, and garlic and cook, stirring, for about 7 minutes. Add the water, split peas, barley, potatoes, parsley, oregano, and pepper and bring to a simmer over medium-high heat. Reduce the heat to medium and cook, stirring occasionally, until the peas are tender, about 1 hour. Stir in the spinach and salt and cook over low heat for 10 to 15 minutes.

Ladle the stew into bowls and serve with warm French bread.

Helpful Tip:

To speed up the cooking time, soak the split peas in water for 1 hour before cooking.

Creole Eggplant and Black-Eyed Pea Stew

A trio of peppery flavors—black pepper, cayenne, and Tabasco sauce—gives this vegetable stew a nice zing of spicy heat.

Yield: 6 servings

2	tablespoons olive oil
4	cups diced eggplant (about 1 medium eggplant)
2	large tomatoes, diced
1	medium yellow onion, diced
1	green bell pepper, seeded and diced
2	cloves garlic, minced
1	can (28 ounces) crushed tomatoes
1	cup water
1	tablespoon dried oregano
2	teaspoons dried thyme leaves
½	teaspoon black pepper
¼	teaspoon ground cayenne
½	teaspoon salt
1	can (15 ounces) black-eyed peas or red kidney beans, drained
1	to 3 teaspoons Tabasco or other bottled hot sauce

In a large saucepan, heat the oil over medium heat. Add the eggplant, tomatoes, onion, bell pepper, and garlic and cook, stirring, over medium heat for about 10 minutes. Add the tomatoes, water, oregano, thyme, pepper, cayenne, and salt and cook over medium-low heat for 25 minutes, stirring occasionally. Stir in the black-eyed peas and Tabasco and cook for 5 minutes. Remove from the heat and let stand for 10 minutes.

Serve the stew with brown rice or other grains, and pass the bottle of Tabasco at the table.

Mexican Green Rice

Called arroz verde in Spanish, this dish is a pleasing combination of roasted chilies, spinach, herbs, and rice. For a variation, try basmati or jasmine rice.

Yield: 4 servings

1½	tablespoons canola oil
1	medium yellow onion, diced
2	cloves garlic, minced
2	roasted poblano chili peppers, seeded and chopped
1	jalapeño chili pepper, seeded and minced
2	cups water
1	cup long-grain white rice
2	to 3 tablespoons chopped fresh parsley
1	teaspoon ground cumin
½	teaspoon salt
¼	teaspoon black pepper
2	cups chopped fresh spinach or other leafy green vegetable
2	tablespoons minced fresh cilantro

In a saucepan, heat the oil over medium heat. Add the onion, garlic, and chili peppers and cook, stirring, for 5 to 7 minutes. Add the water, rice, parsley, cumin, salt, and pepper and bring to a simmer over medium-high heat. Stir the grains, cover, and cook over medium-low heat for about 12 minutes.

Stir in the spinach and cilantro and cook over low heat until the rice is tender, 4 to 5 minutes. Remove from the heat, fluff the rice, and let stand for 5 to 10 minutes before serving.

Stove-Top Quinoa Pilaf

Quinoa (pronounced "keen-wa") is a nutrient-rich grain with a nutty flavor and rice-like texture. It is a perfect ingredient for pilafs, casseroles, and one-pot dishes.

Yield: 4 servings

1	tablespoon canola oil
1	small yellow onion, diced
8	to 10 white mushrooms, sliced
1	green or red bell pepper, seeded and diced
1	small zucchini, diced
2	cups water
1	cup quinoa, rinsed
1	cup peeled, diced butternut squash or sweet potato
2	tablespoons chopped fresh parsley
½	teaspoon black pepper
½	to 1 teaspoon salt

In a large saucepan, heat the oil over medium heat. Add the onion, mushrooms, bell pepper, and zucchini and cook, stirring, for 5 to 7 minutes. Add the water, quinoa, squash, parsley, pepper, and salt and bring to a simmer over medium-high heat. Stir the grains, cover, and cook over medium-low heat until all of the liquid is absorbed, 15 to 20 minutes. Remove from the heat, fluff the grains, and let stand, covered, for 5 to 10 minutes before serving.

Helpful Tip:

Remember to rinse the quinoa in cold water before cooking. It is important to wash away a natural (but bitter-tasting) coating called saponin.

Black Bean–
Jalapeño Succotash

This Native American dish of beans and corn is traditionally prepared with lima beans, but black beans and jalapeños make for an interesting twist. Serve as a side dish.

Yield: 4 servings

1	tablespoon canola oil
1	small yellow onion, finely chopped
1	red or green bell pepper, seeded and diced
2	cloves garlic, minced
1	jalapeño chili pepper, seeded and minced
1	can (14 ounces) corn kernels, drained
1	can (15 ounces) black beans, drained
1	teaspoon dried oregano
½	teaspoon black pepper
½	teaspoon salt
2	to 3 tablespoons chopped fresh cilantro (optional)

In a medium saucepan, heat the oil over medium heat. Add the onion, bell pepper, garlic, and jalapeño and cook, stirring, for 5 minutes. Add the corn, beans, oregano, pepper, and salt and cook for 5 to 7 minutes, stirring occasionally.

Fold in the optional cilantro and serve at once.

"Jump Up" Rice and Beans

This high-spirited side dish is a good choice to serve at a dinner party or casual gathering ("jump up" refers to a Caribbean celebration). Coconut milk gives the rice a nutty nuance.

Yield: 6 servings

1	tablespoon canola oil
1	medium yellow onion, diced
1	red bell pepper, seeded and diced
2	or 3 cloves garlic, minced
½	Scotch bonnet chili pepper, seeded and minced (optional)
3½	cups water
2	cups long-grain white rice
1	can (15 ounces) red kidney beans, drained
½	cup canned coconut milk
2	teaspoons curry powder
½	teaspoon dried thyme
½	teaspoon black pepper
½	teaspoon salt

In a large saucepan, heat the oil over medium heat. Add the onion, bell pepper, garlic, and optional Scotch bonnet chili pepper and cook, stirring, for 5 minutes. Stir in the water, rice, beans, coconut milk, curry powder, thyme, pepper, and salt and bring to a simmer over medium-high heat. Stir the grains, cover the pan, and cook over medium-low heat until all of the liquid is absorbed, 15 to 20 minutes. Remove from the heat, fluff the rice, and let stand, covered, for 5 to 10 minutes before serving.

Spoon the rice onto plates and serve at once.

Powerhouse
Barley Pilaf

This one-pot dish of barley, wild rice, and lentils is packed with comforting flavors and soothing textures.

Yield: 4 servings

1	tablespoon canola oil
1	medium yellow onion, diced
1	red bell pepper, seeded and diced
8	ounces white mushrooms, chopped
3	or 4 cloves garlic, minced
1½	teaspoons curry powder
4	cups water
½	cup pearl barley
¼	cup wild rice
¼	cup green lentils, rinsed
½	teaspoon black pepper
½	teaspoon salt

In a medium saucepan, heat the oil over medium-high heat. Add the onion, bell pepper, mushrooms, and garlic, and cook, stirring, for about 6 minutes. Stir in the curry powder and cook, stirring, for 1 minute. Stir in the water, barley, wild rice, lentils, and pepper and bring to a simmer over medium-heat heat. Cover and cook over medium-low heat until all of the liquid is absorbed, 40 to 45 minutes (stir the grains every 10 minutes or so).

Remove from the heat, fluff the grains, and stir in the salt. Let stand for 5 to 10 minutes before serving.

Red Bean Ratatouille

Adding beans to this tomato-and-eggplant stew is an easy way to increase the protein and fiber content in a meal (while adding flavors as well).

Yield: 4 servings

2	tablespoons canola oil
1	medium yellow onion, diced
1	green bell pepper, seeded and diced
8	ounces white mushrooms, sliced
2	cups diced eggplant
4	cloves garlic, minced
1	can (14 ounces) stewed tomatoes
1	can (14 ounces) tomato puree
1	can (14 ounces) red kidney beans, drained
1	tablespoon dried parsley
2	teaspoons dried oregano
½	teaspoon black pepper
½	teaspoon salt

In a large saucepan, heat the oil over medium heat. Add the onion, bell pepper, mushrooms, eggplant, and garlic and cook over medium heat, stirring, until the vegetables are tender, 8 to 10 minutes. Stir in the tomatoes, tomato puree, beans, parsley, oregano, pepper, and salt and cook over medium-low heat for 15 to 20 minutes, stirring occasionally.

Remove from the heat and serve over pasta or rice.

Lentil, Spinach, and Bulgur Stew

This satisfying cauldron of legumes and grains provides plenty of protein, fiber, and high-energy carbohydrates.

Yield: 3 to 4 servings

1	cup green lentils, rinsed
4½	cups water
½	cup coarse bulgur
½	teaspoon salt
½	teaspoon black pepper
2	cups chopped fresh spinach
1	to 2 tablespoons olive oil
1	medium yellow onion, slivered

In a medium saucepan, combine the lentils and water and bring to a simmer over medium heat. Cook for about 25 minutes, stirring occasionally. Stir in the bulgur, salt, and pepper and cook over medium-low heat, stirring occasionally, until the lentils are tender, 15 to 20 minutes. (Add a little hot water if necessary.) Stir in the spinach, cover, remove from the heat, and set aside for about 10 minutes.

In a large skillet, heat the oil. Add the onion and cook, stirring, until the onions are lightly browned, 7 to 9 minutes. Stir the onions into the stew.

Serve with warm pita bread.

Helpful Tip:

For a tangy version, squeeze 1 or 2
lemons over the stew before serving.

Tofu and Vegetable Tossed Rice

This stir-fry dish is prepared like fried rice—only without the shredded meat and eggs.

Yield: 4 servings

1	tablespoon canola oil
12	to 14 white mushrooms, sliced
1	red bell pepper, seeded and diced
1	medium red onion, diced
1	jalapeño chili pepper, seeded and minced (optional)
½	pound extra-firm tofu, diced
8	to 10 broccoli florets, blanched
4	cups cooked long-grain brown rice or basmati rice
3	to 4 tablespoons soy sauce
1½	teaspoons toasted sesame oil
3	to 4 tablespoons chopped fresh parsley or cilantro

In a large skillet or wok, heat the canola oil over medium-high heat. Add the mushrooms, bell pepper, onion, and optional jalapeño. Cook, stirring, for about 3 minutes. Stir in the tofu and broccoli and cook, stirring, for about 5 minutes. Stir in the rice, soy sauce, and sesame oil, reduce the heat to medium, and cook, stirring, until the rice is steaming, about 4 minutes.

Spoon the rice and tofu mixture onto serving plates and sprinkle the parsley over the top. Serve at once.

Helpful Tips:

Add 1 tablespoon minced fresh ginger root along with the vegetables. Zucchini, corn, or snow peas can also be included in the stir-fry.

Black Bean–
Tofu Chili

This boisterous, highly seasoned chili will be a sure winner when served as a first course.

Yield: 6 servings

1	tablespoon canola oil
1	medium yellow onion, diced
1	green bell pepper, seeded and diced
2	celery stalks, chopped
2	or 3 cloves garlic, minced
1	can (28 ounces) crushed tomatoes
1	can (15 ounces) black beans, drained
½	cup water
½	pound extra-firm tofu, diced
1½	tablespoons chili powder
1	tablespoon dried parsley
1	tablespoon dried oregano
2	teaspoons ground cumin
½	teaspoon black pepper
½	teaspoon salt

In a large saucepan, heat the oil over medium-high heat. Add the onion, bell pepper, celery, and garlic and cook, stirring, for 5 to 7 minutes. Stir in the tomatoes, beans, water, tofu, chili powder, parsley, oregano, cumin, pepper, and salt. Reduce the heat to medium-low and cook, uncovered, for 20 to 25 minutes, stirring occasionally. Remove the chili from the heat and let stand for 5 to 10 minutes before serving.

Serve with warm bread or corn bread.

Multivegetable Couscous

This colorful mélange of vegetables and couscous makes a light dinner or quick side dish.

Yield: 4 servings

1	tablespoon canola oil
1	medium yellow onion, diced
1	red bell pepper, seeded and diced
2	large cloves garlic, minced
3	cups water
3	cups coarsely chopped fresh spinach or green chard
2	teaspoons dried oregano
½	teaspoon salt
½	teaspoon black pepper
2	cups couscous
1	can (15 ounces) chick-peas, drained
4	whole scallions, trimmed and chopped
	Juice of 1 large lemon or lime

In a large saucepan, heat the oil over medium-high heat. Add the onion, bell pepper, and garlic and cook, stirring, for about 5 minutes. Add the water, spinach, oregano, salt, and pepper and bring to a simmer. Cook, stirring, for 3 to 4 minutes. Stir in the couscous, chick-peas, and scallions, cover, and remove from the heat. Let stand for 10 minutes.

Fluff the couscous and fold in the lemon juice. Serve at once.

Black Bean and
Brown Rice Jambalaya

*Here is delicious proof that jambalaya does not require
sausage, poultry, or meat. This healthy adaptation is hearty,
robust, and filled with good-for-you staples.*

Yield: 6 servings

1½	cups brown rice
3¼	cups water
1	tablespoon canola oil
8	ounces white mushrooms, sliced
1	green bell pepper, seeded and diced
1	medium yellow onion, diced
1	large celery stalk, diced
3	or 4 cloves garlic, minced
1	can (15 ounces) tomato puree
1	can (14 ounces) stewed tomatoes
1	can (15 ounces) black beans, drained
1	tablespoon dried oregano
½	teaspoon black pepper
½	teaspoon ground cayenne
1	to 2 teaspoons bottled hot sauce (such as Tabasco)

In a medium saucepan, combine the rice and water and bring
to a simmer over medium-high heat. Stir the rice, cover the
pan, and cook over medium-low heat until all of the liquid is

absorbed, 30 to 35 minutes. Remove from the heat and let stand for 5 to 10 minutes.

In a large saucepan, heat the oil over medium heat. Add the mushrooms, bell pepper, onion, celery, and garlic and cook, stirring, for 7 to 8 minutes. Add the tomato puree, tomatoes, beans, oregano, pepper, cayenne, and hot sauce and cook over medium-low heat for 15 minutes, stirring occasionally. Fold in the cooked rice and cook over low heat, stirring, for 4 to 6 minutes.

Ladle the jambalaya into wide bowls and serve at once.

Indian Lentils with Curried Potatoes

This energetically spiced dish of luscious lentils and pungent curry has a smooth, pureed consistency. Serve it as a side dish or warm dip.

Yield: 4 to 6 servings

1	tablespoon canola oil
1	large yellow onion, chopped
3	or 4 cloves garlic, minced
1	large tomato, diced
1	tablespoon curry powder
½	teaspoon ground cumin
½	teaspoon black pepper
¼	teaspoon ground turmeric
1	cup green lentils, rinsed
4½	cups water
2	cups peeled, diced white potatoes
½	teaspoon salt

In a medium saucepan, heat the oil over medium heat. Add the onion and garlic and cook, stirring, for about 5 minutes. Stir in the tomato, curry powder, cumin, pepper, and turmeric and cook for 1 minute. Stir in the lentils and water and cook over medium heat for 15 minutes, stirring occasionally. Stir in the potatoes and cook until the lentils and potatoes are tender, about 30 minutes, stirring occasionally. Stir in the salt, remove from the heat, and let stand for 5 to 10 minutes.

Transfer the lentils to a large serving bowl. Serve with Indian flat bread, pita bread, or flour tortillas.

Helpful Tip:

For a touch of heat, add 1 or 2 hot chili peppers (seeded and minced) while sautéing the onion and garlic.

Super Bowl of Chili

This festive dish is exuberantly spiced, unpretentious, and a breeze to make. For maximum fun, serve a selection of toppings, such as chopped scallions, red onions, and sliced avocados.

Yield: 4 to 6 servings

1	tablespoon canola oil
1	large yellow onion, diced
2	green or red bell peppers, seeded and diced
2	stalks celery, diced
4	cloves garlic, minced
1	can (28 ounces) crushed tomatoes
1	can (15 ounces) red kidney beans, drained
1	can (14 ounces) stewed tomatoes
1	tablespoon chili powder
1	tablespoon dried oregano
2	teaspoons ground cumin
1	teaspoon paprika
1	teaspoon salt
1	to 2 teaspoons Tabasco or other bottled hot sauce
½	teaspoon black pepper

In a large saucepan, heat the oil over medium-high heat. Add the onion, bell peppers, celery, and garlic and cook, stirring, for 6 to 8 minutes. Stir in the crushed tomatoes, beans, stewed tomatoes, chili powder, oregano, cumin, paprika, salt, Tabasco, and pepper and bring to a simmer over medium-high heat. Reduce the heat to low and cook, uncovered, for 25 to 30 minutes, stirring occasionally. Remove from the heat and let stand for 5 to 10 minutes before serving.

Ladle the chili into bowls and serve with corn bread or whole wheat bread.

Curried Chick-Peas with Potatoes

This simple dish of chick-peas and potatoes exudes assertive curry flavors.

Yield: 4 servings

1	tablespoon canola oil
1	medium yellow onion, diced
1	large ripe tomato, diced
2	cloves garlic, minced
1	jalapeño or other hot chili pepper, seeded and minced
1	tablespoon dried parsley
2	to 3 teaspoons curry powder
1½	teaspoons ground cumin
1	teaspoon salt
½	teaspoon black pepper
2	cups peeled, diced white potatoes
2	cups water
1	can (15 ounces) chick-peas, drained

In a large saucepan, heat the oil over medium-high heat. Add the onion, tomato, garlic, and jalapeño and cook, stirring, for 5 minutes. Stir in the parsley, curry powder, cumin, salt, and pepper, reduce the heat to low, and cook, stirring, for 1 minute. Add the potatoes and water and bring to a simmer over medium-high heat. Reduce the heat to medium-low and cook for 15 minutes, stirring occasionally. Stir in the chick-peas and cook until the potatoes are tender, 10 to 15 minutes. To thicken, mash some of the potatoes against the side of the pan with the back of a large spoon.

Serve the curried vegetables over rice or other grains.

Pumpkin Rice and Red Beans

This side dish is traditionally made with West Indian pumpkin, a huge squash with a vibrant, sweet potato–like flesh. Butternut or red kuri squash can be substituted.

Yield: 4 servings

1	tablespoon canola oil
1	medium yellow onion, chopped
2	large cloves garlic, minced
2	cups peeled, diced West Indian pumpkin or butternut squash
2	teaspoons curry powder
½	teaspoon black pepper
½	teaspoon salt
¼	teaspoon ground cloves
3	cups water
1½	cups white long-grain rice or basmati rice
1	cup shredded fresh kale or spinach
1	can (15 ounces) red kidney beans, drained

In a large saucepan, heat the oil over medium heat. Add the onion and garlic and cook, stirring, for 5 minutes. Stir in the pumpkin, curry powder, pepper, salt, and cloves and cook for 1 minute.

Add the water, rice, kale, and beans. Stir the grains and bring to a simmer over medium-high heat. Cover and cook over medium-low heat until all of the liquid is absorbed, about 18 minutes. Remove from the heat, fluff the rice, and let stand for 10 minutes before serving.

Savory Squash Pilaf

Butternut squash and rice team up to form this incredibly easy (yet flavorful) side dish.

Yield: 4 servings

1	tablespoon canola oil
1	medium red onion, chopped
2	cloves garlic, minced
3	cups water
2	cups diced butternut squash or other winter squash
1½	cups long-grain white rice or brown rice
½	teaspoon black pepper
½	teaspoon salt
3	or 4 tablespoons chopped fresh parsley

In a medium saucepan, heat the oil over medium heat. Add the onion and garlic and cook, stirring, for 4 minutes. Stir in the water, squash, rice, pepper, and salt and bring to a simmer over medium-high heat. Stir the grains, cover the pan, and cook over low heat until all of the liquid is absorbed, 15 to 20 minutes. (If using brown rice, add ¼ cup more water and cook for 30 to 35 minutes.)

Fluff the grains and stir in the parsley. Replace the cover, remove from the heat, and let stand for 5 to 10 minutes before serving.

Sweet Potato Pilaf

Adding sweet potatoes to a pilaf is a clever and simple way to include carotene-rich vegetables into your meal.

Yield: 4 servings

1	tablespoon canola oil
1	medium yellow onion, diced
8	to 10 button mushrooms, chopped
2	cloves garlic, minced
3	cups water
1	medium sweet potato, peeled and diced
1	cup long-grain brown rice
½	teaspoon salt
½	teaspoon black pepper
½	teaspoon ground turmeric or curry powder
½	cup orzo
2	whole scallions, trimmed and chopped

In a large saucepan, heat the oil over medium heat. Add the onion, mushrooms, and garlic and cook, stirring, for 5 minutes. Stir in the water, sweet potato, rice, salt, pepper, and turmeric and bring to a simmer over medium-high heat. Stir the grains, add the orzo, and cover the pan. Reduce the heat to medium-low and cook until all of the liquid is absorbed, 30 to 35 minutes.

Remove from the heat and fluff the grains. Stir in the scallions and let stand for about 10 minutes before serving.

Helpful Tip:

Orzo, also called rosa maria, is a rice-shaped pasta sold in the pasta section of grocery stores.

Jasmine Rice and Black Bean Burritos

Jasmine rice has a nutty, popcornlike flavor and soft texture. It makes a great filling for this vegetable and bean burrito.

Yield: 4 burritos

1	cup jasmine rice
2	cups water
½	teaspoon ground turmeric
½	teaspoon black pepper
½	teaspoon salt
1	tablespoon canola oil
1	medium yellow onion, diced
1	green or red bell pepper, seeded and diced
1	medium zucchini, diced
1	can (15 ounces) black beans, drained
4	(10-inch) flour tortillas
½	cup tomato salsa or guacamole

In a medium saucepan, combine the rice, water, turmeric, pepper, and salt and bring to a simmer over medium-high heat. Stir the rice, cover the pan, and cook over medium-low heat for 12 to 15 minutes. Remove from the heat, fluff the grains, replace the cover, and let stand for 5 minutes.

In a medium saucepan, heat the oil over medium-high heat. Add the onion, bell pepper, and zucchini and cook, stirring, for 6 minutes. Stir in the beans and cook, stirring, for 2 minutes. Fold in the cooked rice and cover. Remove from heat and set aside until the tortillas are warm.

Warm the tortillas over a hot burner or pan and place on large serving plates. Spoon the rice and bean mixture down the center of each tortilla. Roll the tortillas around the filling. Spoon the salsa or guacamole over the top of the burritos and serve at once.

Yellow Rice and Avocado Burritos

Avocados lend a creamy texture to this savory, well-filled burrito, and the turmeric gives it a yellow hue.

Yield: 4 burritos

1	cup long-grain white rice
2	cups water
½	teaspoon ground turmeric
½	teaspoon black pepper
½	teaspoon salt
1	can (15 ounces) pinto beans, drained
½	cup diced roasted red peppers
1	ripe avocado, peeled, pitted, and diced
2	whole scallions, trimmed and chopped
4	(10-inch) flour tortillas
½	cup tomato salsa

In a medium saucepan, combine the rice, water, turmeric, pepper, and salt and bring to a simmer over medium-high heat. Stir the rice, cover the pan, and cook over medium-low heat for 12 to 15 minutes. Remove from the heat, fluff the grains, and fold in the beans, roasted peppers, avocado, and scallions. Replace the cover and let stand for 5 to 10 minutes.

Warm the tortillas over a hot burner or pan and place on large serving plates. Spoon the rice mixture down the center of each tortilla. Roll the tortillas around the filling. Spoon the salsa on the side of the burritos and serve at once.

Helpful Tip:

Roasted red peppers are available in jars in the relish/pickle section of grocery stores.

Black Bean Refritos

Refritos loosely means "well cooked" in Spanish. In this recipe, the beans are fully cooked, pureed or mashed, and briefly cooked again. Using canned beans speeds up the process. Serve the beans as a side dish (or filling) for burritos or quesadillas.

Yield: 6 servings

2	cans (15 ounces each) black beans
1	tablespoon canola oil
1	medium yellow onion, diced
2	large cloves garlic, minced
1	tablespoon chopped pickled jalapeños (optional)
1	tablespoon dried oregano
½	teaspoon black pepper
½	teaspoon salt

Drain the canned beans, reserving ½ cup of the liquid.

In a medium saucepan, heat the oil. Add the onion and garlic and cook, stirring, for 4 minutes over medium-high heat. Add the beans and liquid, optional jalapeños, oregano, pepper, and salt and cook over medium-low heat, stirring, for 8 minutes.

Transfer the bean mixture to a blender and process until smooth, about 5 seconds, stopping to stir the beans at least once. Return the mixture to the pan and cook over low heat, stirring, for about 5 minutes. Serve at once.

Maple Amaranth with Wheat Germ

This delicious hot breakfast (or late-night snack) is reminiscent of oatmeal. Amaranth has a nutty flavor and creamy texture.

Yield: 3 to 4 servings

1	cup amaranth
3	cups water
3	to 4 tablespoons maple syrup
2	tablespoons wheat germ

In a medium saucepan, combine the amaranth with water and bring to a simmer over medium heat. Reduce the heat to medium-low and cook for 20 to 25 minutes, stirring occasionally, until the grains become thick and soft.

Spoon the amaranth into bowls and swirl in 1 tablespoonful the maple syrup into each bowl. Sprinkle the wheat germ over the top and serve at once.

Helpful Tip:

For additional nutrients and flavor, add diced fruit (such as apples, pears, and peaches) to the simmering amaranth.

Chapter 6

---◆---

Dig This Trio
Potatoes, Squash, and Root Vegetables

Potatoes, winter squash, and root vegetables can all be described in one word: versatile. This trio of hardy vegetables can be baked, boiled, roasted, mashed, steamed, and barbecued. Countless soups, stews, and one-pot dishes owe their soothing textures and stick-to-your-ribs substance to these humble pantry staples.

Potato Possibilities

The ever-expanding selection of potatoes includes long whites, reds, sweet potatoes (not really potatoes, but roots), Yukon golds, all-purpose, and exotic blue potatoes. Although most potatoes are interchangeable, they are grouped by their starch content. **High-starch potatoes,** such as russets, have a "floury" flavor and fluffy texture and make the best baked potatoes. **Medium-starch potatoes,** such as all-purpose or boiling potatoes, hold up well in boiled water and can be baked, mashed, roasted, or added to soups or salads. **Low-starch potatoes,** such as Yukon gold and new potatoes, have a firm, waxy texture and are great for salads and barbecuing.

Always store potatoes in a cool, dark place. Direct sunshine or heat will hasten the demise of a good potato. Never refrigerate potatoes. The high-energy starches will turn to sugars. Never store potatoes in plastic bags (tubers need to breathe). Store potatoes in either a brown paper bag or loosely piled in a plastic bin. Discard any potatoes covered with a potentially toxic green hue. Also, remove any sprouts and blemishes before cooking.

A World of Winter Squash

Winter squash come in a variety of shapes, sizes, and colors. Despite their name, "winter" squash are available throughout most of the year (they are also called hard-shelled squash). Winter squash are healthful, easy to prepare, and interchangeable in most recipes. The sturdy gourds are good sources of beta-carotene, vitamin C, potassium, and fiber. Winter squash are also low in calories, sodium, and fat.

There are a few tips to cooking with winter squash. First, when choosing a winter squash, look for hard, firm shells that are free of blemishes, soft spots, or broken skins. Pick up and hold the squash; it should feel heavy and dense. To roast a large squash, cut the gourd in half with a sharp knife and remove the seeds and stringy fiber. Place the squash in a baking pan filled with about ¼ inch of water and roast in an oven at

375 degrees F, until the pulp is easily pierced with a fork, 30 to 40 minutes.

Most winter squash are available in well-stocked supermarkets, natural food stores, and ethnic markets. If kept in a cool, dark place and away from sunlight, winter squash will keep for several months. Here is a broad overview of some popular varieties of the winter gourd family.

Acorn squash are shaped like a large acorn with pleated ridges. The dark green gourds are naturally decorated with sporadic streaks of golden orange and yellow. Easy to roast, acorn's flesh is mild and soft.

Blue hubbard is so large that it is often sold in wedges. It has a pale bluish-gray skin and a surprisingly vibrant orange flesh. Blue hubbard tastes somewhat like a butternut squash or West Indian pumpkin.

Buttercup squash are dark green gourds with portly, rotund shapes. The bronze-orange flesh is mildly sweet and buttery and can be roasted like acorn squash.

Butternut are the most versatile winter squash and are widely available. The squash have long, tan necks and bell-shaped, bulbous ends where seeds are stored. The orange flesh has a sweetness similar to sweet potato and melds easily into soups, grain and rice dishes, risotto, and sauces.

Delicata are sometimes called sweet potato squash. They have a sweet, yellowish-orange flesh and are treasured for their buttery flavors. The small, elongated squash have ribbed skins and green, white, or orange streaks. Roasted delicata usually make one serving.

Kabocha are cherished in Japanese cuisine. The rotund, dark green gourds have a dense orange flesh and a sweet-and-savory taste. Kabocha can be roasted like acorn squash.

Pumpkin refers to two main varieties: small sugar pie and large field pumpkins (jack-o'-lanterns). Sugar pie pumpkins have a dense, rich flesh and are commonly used for cooking. Field pumpkins are mildly flavored and seedy and are often used as Halloween ornaments. For convenience, canned pumpkin is a good kitchen staple (and contains concentrated amounts of beta-carotene).

Red kuri squash, also called golden hubbard, is a large, reddish-orange squash with a thin skin and delectable flesh. Similar in flavor to blue hubbard and West Indian pumpkin, red kuri is a farmers' market staple and widely available in autumn.

Sugar loaf and **sweet dumpling** are small, sweet-tasting squash similar to delicata in flavor. The squash are interchangeable with delicata and acorn squash and can be roasted and served as a single serving.

West Indian pumpkin, also called calabaza, is a huge, gigantic gourd with a bold orange, sweet-tasting flesh. The skin varies from tan and orange to streaky forest green. The shape can be round like sugar pie pumpkins or elongated and heavy like watermelons. West Indian pumpkin is often sold in precut wedges in Caribbean and Hispanic markets; it is occasionally available in well-stocked supermarkets or natural food stores.

Dig Those Root Vegetables

Humble root vegetables inspire a bounty of imaginative, hearty dishes perfect for any time of year. Root vegetables can be julienned, diced, grated, roasted, mashed and smashed, or added to soups and stews. They meld well with a spectrum of ingredients, from garlic, chili peppers, and curries to subtle herbs, sweet spices, and tart vinegars. As a whole, root vegetables are inexpensive, widely available, and easy to prepare and have a long storage life.

Here is a sampling of "root cellar" vegetables:

Beet roots have the versatility of potato and the crisp flavor of a vegetable. Look for magenta beets with their green tops still attached—the beet greens are an added bonus. Beets can be shredded raw and tossed into a salad or roasted whole and lightly dressed. They are best known for their role in borscht, the Russian bisque.

Carrots are nutritional powerhouses, loaded with carotenoids, vitamin C, fiber, and other nutrients. Add carrots to soups, stews, marinaras, pilafs, and myriad other one-pot dishes.

Parsnip roots look like an albino carrot. Parsnips have a mild, slightly sweet, starchy flavor with a firm, crunchy texture. Try using it in place of a potato.

Rutabagas are large, softball-sized, earth-toned orbs with a firm yellowish flesh and a mild cauliflower-like flavor. The bulbous root is covered with a thin coat of wax (paraffin) that extends its shelf life; it should be peeled before cooking.

Turnips are roundish, off-white orbs with a light purple band around the top. They have a firm texture and subtle radish flavor. The greens are edible as well.

Soy-Mashed Potatoes

For this nouveau bowl of mashed potatoes, soy milk makes a nutritious replacement for heavy cream, milk, and/or butter.

Yield: 4 servings

2½	quarts water
4	cups peeled, diced white potatoes
½	cup soy milk, warmed
¼	cup chopped fresh parsley
½	teaspoon white pepper
½	teaspoon salt
2	large whole scallions, finely chopped

In a large saucepan, bring the water to a boil. Add the potatoes and cook over medium heat until tender, about 20 minutes, stirring occasionally. Drain in a colander.

Transfer the potatoes to a medium mixing bowl. Add the soy milk, parsley, pepper, and salt to the potatoes and mash with the back of a large spoon or potato masher until pureed.

Transfer to a serving bowl and sprinkle the scallions over the top. Serve at once.

Gourmet Squash with Maple Syrup

Gourmet winter squash are easy to prepare and are good sources of carotenoids, fiber, and essential nutrients. Some favorite varieties include delicata, sweet dumpling, buttercup, and sugar loaf. Serve as a healthy side dish.

Yield: 4 servings

3	or 4 delicata squash or other small winter squash
½	cup soy milk, warmed
1	to 2 tablespoons maple syrup
¼	teaspoon ground nutmeg
¼	teaspoon white pepper

Preheat the oven to 400 degrees F.

Cut the squash in half lengthwise and scoop out the seeds and stringy fibers. Place the squash cut side down on a sheet pan filled with about ¼ inch of water. Bake for 25 to 35 minutes until the flesh is tender (easily pierced with a fork). Remove the squash from the oven, flip over, and let cool for 5 to 10 minutes.

When the squash has cooled, scoop out the pulp and transfer to a medium mixing bowl. Add the soy milk, maple syrup, nutmeg, and pepper; mash the mixture as you would potatoes. Serve at once.

West Indian Pumpkin Sancocho

Sancocho is the name of a hearty Caribbean stew. This meatless version features potatoes, carrots, and West Indian pumpkin, a huge gourd with a vibrant orange flesh and sweet flavor.

Yield: 4 servings

1	tablespoon canola oil
1	medium yellow onion, diced
1	green bell pepper, seeded and diced
2	cloves garlic, minced
1	jalapeño or other hot chili pepper, seeded and minced
1	large tomato, diced
1½	tablespoons dried parsley
2	teaspoons curry powder
1½	teaspoons ground cumin
1	teaspoon dried thyme
½	teaspoon black pepper
½	teaspoon salt
4	cups water
2	medium carrots, peeled and diced
2	cups peeled, diced white potatoes
2	cups peeled, diced West Indian pumpkin

In a large saucepan, heat the oil over medium heat. Add the onion, bell pepper, garlic, and jalapeño and cook, stirring, for 5 minutes. Stir in the tomato, parsley, curry powder, cumin, thyme, pepper, and salt and cook, stirring, for 2 minutes over low heat. Add the water, carrots, potatoes, and pumpkin and bring to a simmer. Cook over medium-low heat, stirring occasionally, until the vegetables are tender, 40 to 45 minutes. Remove from the heat and let stand for 5 to 10 minutes before serving. To thicken, mash the pumpkin and potatoes against the side of the pan with the back of a large spoon.

Ladle into bowls and serve with warm bread.

Helpful Tip:

Look for West Indian pumpkin (also called calabaza) in Caribbean and Hispanic markets or in well-stocked supermarkets. Butternut squash can be substituted.

Porotos Granados

This South American version of comfort food includes three native New World crops: pumpkin, corn, and beans. Porotos granados loosely means "choice beans."

Yield: 4 to 6 servings

1	tablespoon canola oil
1	medium yellow onion, diced
2	or 3 cloves garlic, minced
1	jalapeño chili pepper, seeded and minced
2	large tomatoes, diced
1	tablespoon paprika
1½	tablespoons dried parsley
2	teaspoons dried oregano
1	teaspoon ground cumin
½	teaspoon black pepper
½	teaspoon salt
4	cups peeled, diced pumpkin or butternut squash
4	cups water
1	can (14 ounces) corn kernels, drained
1	can (15 ounces) cranberry beans or red kidney beans, drained

In a large saucepan, heat the oil over medium heat. Add the onion, garlic, and jalapeño and cook, stirring, for about 4 minutes. Add the tomatoes, paprika, parsley, oregano, cumin, pepper, and salt and cook, stirring, for 3 to 4 minutes. Add the pumpkin and water and bring to a simmer over medium-high heat. Reduce the heat to medium-low and cook until the pumpkin is tender, about 30 minutes, stirring occasionally. Stir in the corn and beans and cook for about 10 minutes over low heat. To thicken, mash the pumpkin against the side of the pan with the back of a large spoon.

Serve the stew with a side of quinoa or brown rice.

Rosemary-Roasted Jerusalem Artichokes

Go figure—Jerusalem artichokes are neither artichokes nor from Jerusalem. Rather, the knobby tubers are indigenous to North America and belong to the sunflower family (they are also called sun chokes, a more appropriate name). Serve as a side dish to pilafs, stews, or other one-pot dishes.

Yield: 4 servings

4	to 6 cloves garlic
1½	tablespoons olive oil
2	teaspoons dried rosemary *or*
	1 tablespoon chopped fresh rosemary
1½	pounds Jerusalem artichokes,
	scrubbed and halved
	About ½ teaspoon paprika
	Salt and ground black pepper, to taste

Preheat the oven to 400 degrees F.

Combine the garlic, oil, and rosemary in a mixing bowl. Toss in the Jerusalem artichokes and coat with the mixture. Place the garlic cloves and Jerusalem artichokes, cut sides down, on a baking pan. Lightly sprinkle the paprika over the top and place in the oven. Bake until the Jerusalem artichokes are tender but not mushy, 30 to 40 minutes.

Transfer the tubers to a serving platter and season with salt and pepper. Garnish with fresh sprigs of rosemary or other herbs.

Moroccan Squash and Couscous Stew

Winter squash blends well with fluffy couscous, the grainlike pasta prevalent in Moroccan and North African cuisine. This stew is heightened with harissa, an aromatic spice paste with an intense level of heat.

Yield: 4 to 6 servings

1	tablespoon canola oil
1	medium yellow onion, diced
1	red bell pepper, seeded and diced
2	or 3 cloves garlic, minced
2	large ripe tomatoes, diced
1½	to 2 tablespoons harissa
4	cups water
2	cups peeled, diced butternut squash
½	teaspoon salt
1	can (15 ounces) chick-peas, drained
½	cup couscous
2	to 3 tablespoons chopped fresh parsley

In a large saucepan, heat the oil over medium heat. Add the onion, bell pepper, and garlic and cook, stirring, for 4 minutes. Add the tomatoes and cook, stirring, for 2 minutes. Stir in the harissa and cook for 1 minute. Stir in the water, squash, and salt and bring to a simmer over high heat. Reduce the heat to medium-low and cook, stirring occasionally, until the squash is tender, about 25 minutes.

Stir in the chick-peas, couscous, and parsley and cover. Remove from the heat and let stand for 10 to 12 minutes before serving.

Stir the stew and ladle into bowls.

Helpful Tip:

Harissa is available in the specialty
section of well-stocked supermarkets.

Curried Squash with Chick-Peas

For this fragrant and highly spiced stew, butternut squash teams up with ginger, garlic, and potent curry spices. Rice makes a natural companion to the dish.

Yield: 4 servings

1	tablespoon canola oil
1	medium red onion, diced
2	large cloves garlic, minced
2	to 3 teaspoons minced fresh ginger root
1	jalapeño or other hot chili pepper, seeded and minced
2	medium tomatoes, diced
1	tablespoon curry powder
1	teaspoon ground cumin
½	teaspoon black pepper
½	teaspoon salt
¼	teaspoon ground turmeric
2½	to 3 cups peeled, diced butternut squash
2	cups water
1	can (15 ounces) chick-peas, drained

In a large saucepan, heat the oil over medium-high heat. Add the onion, garlic, ginger, and jalapeño and cook, stirring, for

3 minutes. Add the tomatoes and cook, stirring, for 3 to 4 minutes. Stir in the curry powder, cumin, pepper, salt, and turmeric and cook for 1 minute.

Add the squash, water, and chick-peas and bring to a simmer over medium-high heat. Lower the heat to medium and cook, stirring occasionally, until the squash is tender, 20 to 25 minutes. To thicken, mash the squash against the side of the pan with the back of a spoon. Remove from the heat and let stand for 5 minutes before serving.

Serve the curried squash over rice or other grains.

Oven-Roasted Sweet Plantains

Plantains, while not technically a tuber or root vegetable, are a popular starch in African, Caribbean, and Hispanic kitchens. When green plantains ripen, they turn yellowish and black. Despite their appearance, ripe plantains are very desirable, tender, and banana-like. Serve as a side dish to barbecued dishes, pilafs, or other one-pot dishes.

Yield: 4 servings

2	or 3 large yellow plantains
¼	teaspoon ground nutmeg, allspice, or cinnamon

Preheat the oven to 400 degrees F.

Cut off the tips of the plantains. Place the plantains on a baking sheet and bake until the skin is charred and puffy, 15 to 20 minutes.

Remove the plantains from the oven and let cool for a few minutes. Slice the plantains down the center lengthwise and peel back the skin. Cut the plantains in half widthwise, sprinkle with nutmeg, and transfer to serving plates.

Helpful Tip:

To ripen a green plantain, store it at room temperature for five to seven days. Storing the plantains in a paper bag will speed up the ripening process (do not refrigerate). Since most of the plantains in stores are green, it's a good idea to buy them a few days ahead of time.

Curried Potatoes with Spinach

Serve this curried potato stew over a big bowl of rice, as you would with Cajun gumbo.

Yield: 6 servings

1	tablespoon canola oil
1	medium yellow onion, diced
1	large stalk celery, sliced
2	teaspoons minced fresh ginger root
1	large tomato, diced
1	tablespoon curry powder
1	teaspoon garam masala or ground coriander
½	teaspoon salt
¼	teaspoon ground cayenne
4	cups water
2½	cups peeled, diced white potatoes
2	medium carrots, diced
4	cups coarsely chopped spinach
4	cups cooked brown rice or basmati rice

In a large saucepan, heat the oil over medium heat. Add the onion, celery, and ginger and cook, stirring, for about 4 minutes. Add the tomato, curry powder, garam masala, salt, and cayenne and cook, stirring, for 3 minutes over low heat.

Add the water, potatoes, and carrots and cook for 15 minutes over medium heat, stirring occasionally. Stir in the spinach and cook until the potatoes are tender, 10 to 15 minutes, stirring occasionally. Remove from the heat and let stand for about 5 minutes.

To serve, place about ½ cup of the cooked rice into shallow bowls and ladle the curried potatoes over the top.

Herb-Roasted Root Vegetables

Roasting is a great way to bring out the essential (and underrated) flavors of root vegetables. Serve as a side dish to barbecued dishes, pilafs, or other one-pot dishes.

Yield: 6 servings

1	large sweet potato, coarsely chopped
1	large rutabaga, peeled and diced
1	large parsnip, peeled and diced
2	medium turnips, diced
4	to 6 cloves garlic, peeled
3	to 4 tablespoons canola oil
1	tablespoon dried thyme leaves
½	teaspoon salt
½	teaspoon black pepper
1	small bunch fresh thyme sprigs

Preheat the oven to 375 degrees F.

In a mixing bowl, toss the sweet potato, rutabaga, parsnip, turnips, garlic, oil, dried thyme, salt, pepper, and half of the fresh thyme sprigs. Let stand for 10 minutes.

Place the vegetables in a casserole dish or baking pan. Place in the oven and roast until the vegetables are tender, about 1 hour (stir the vegetables every 20 minutes or so).

Remove the vegetables from the oven and let cool slightly before serving. Place the vegetables on a platter and arrange the remaining fresh thyme sprigs around the edges.

Helpful Tips:

Other vegetables, such as carrots, Jerusalem artichokes, large mushrooms, or quartered onions, can also be roasted with the roots. For a light touch at the finish, drizzle a little balsamic vinegar over the roasted vegetables.

Indian Lentils with Sweet Potatoes

Red lentils meld smoothly with potatoes in this curry- and ginger-flavored side dish. It can also be served as a dip with Indian flat bread or flour tortillas.

Yield: 6 servings

2	teaspoons canola oil
1	medium yellow onion, finely chopped
2	large cloves garlic, minced
2	teaspoons minced fresh ginger root
1½	teaspoons curry powder
1	teaspoon ground cumin
¼	teaspoon ground turmeric
½	teaspoon black pepper
1	cup red lentils, rinsed
4	cups water
2	cups peeled, diced sweet potatoes
½	teaspoon salt
4	to 6 rounds Indian flat bread (roti or nan) or pita bread

In a large saucepan, heat the oil over medium heat. Add the onion and garlic and cook, stirring, for 4 minutes. Stir in the ginger, curry powder, cumin, turmeric, and pepper and cook for 30 seconds. Stir in the lentils and water and bring to a simmer over medium-high heat. Reduce the heat to medium-low and cook (uncovered) for 15 minutes, stirring occasionally. Stir in the sweet potatoes and cook for 30 to 40 minutes, stirring occasionally, until the lentils and potatoes are tender. Stir in the salt.

Transfer to a large serving bowl. Serve with Indian flat bread or warm flour tortillas.

Artichoke, Potato, and White Bean Stew

This is an artichoke lover's meal—it's full of delicious flavors and savory textures.

Yield: 6 servings

1	tablespoon canola oil
1	medium yellow onion, diced
1	large stalk celery, chopped
2	cloves garlic, minced
6	cups water
2	medium carrots, peeled and diced
2	cups peeled, diced white potatoes
¼	cup dry white wine
1	tablespoon dried parsley
1	teaspoon salt
½	teaspoon black pepper
1	can (14 ounces) artichoke hearts, drained and coarsely chopped
1	can (15 ounces) white kidney beans, drained
2	to 3 tablespoons chopped fresh parsley
2	lemons, quartered

In a large saucepan, heat the oil over medium heat. Add the onion, celery, and garlic and cook, stirring, for 5 minutes. Add the water, carrots, potatoes, wine, parsley, salt, and pepper and bring to a simmer over high heat. Reduce the heat to medium-low and cook for about 15 minutes, stirring occasionally. Stir in the artichokes and beans and cook for 15 to 20 minutes over low heat, stirring occasionally. Stir in the parsley and squeeze half of the lemon wedges into the stew. Remove from the heat and let stand for 10 minutes before serving.

Ladle the stew into bowls and serve with French bread. Pass the extra lemon at the table.

West African Groundnut Stew

In African cuisine, groundnuts (better known as peanuts) are pureed into pastes (like peanut butter) and added to soups, sauces, and stews. This nutty stew is enhanced with ginger, tomatoes, and sweet potato.

Yield: 6 servings

1	tablespoon canola oil
1	medium yellow onion, diced
1	yellow or red bell pepper, seeded and diced
2	cloves garlic, minced
2	teaspoons minced fresh ginger root
1	jalapeño chili pepper, seeded and minced
2	cups water
2	cups tomato juice
1	can (14 ounces) stewed tomatoes
1	medium sweet potato, peeled and diced
1	tablespoon dried parsley
1½	teaspoons dried thyme
1½	teaspoons ground cumin
½	teaspoon salt
½	cup chunky peanut butter
2	cups shredded spinach

In a large saucepan, heat the oil over medium heat. Add the onion, bell pepper, garlic, ginger, and jalapeño and cook, stirring, for 5 minutes. Stir in the water, tomato juice, tomatoes, sweet potato, parsley, thyme, cumin, and salt and bring to a simmer over medium-high heat. Reduce the heat to medium-low and cook for 20 to 25 minutes until the potatoes are tender, stirring occasionally.

Add the peanut butter and stir until it is completely blended. Stir in the spinach and return to a gentle simmer, stirring frequently. Remove from the heat and let stand for 5 minutes before serving.

Ladle the stew into bowls and serve with couscous or rice.

Spinach Hash Browns

Although these twice-cooked potatoes with spinach are a natural entree for breakfast, they also can be served as a side dish for dinner.

Yield: 3 to 4 servings

4	cups peeled, diced white potatoes
1	tablespoon canola oil
1	small yellow onion, chopped
2	cloves garlic, minced
2	to 3 cups chopped spinach
2	whole scallions, trimmed and chopped
1	teaspoon paprika
1	to 2 teaspoons bottled hot sauce (optional)
½	teaspoon salt
¼	teaspoon ground cayenne

Place the potatoes in boiling water to cover and cook over medium heat until tender, 15 to 20 minutes. Drain the potatoes in a colander.

In a large skillet, heat the oil over medium-high heat. Add the onion and garlic and cook, stirring, for 5 minutes. Stir in the potatoes, spinach, scallions, paprika, optional hot sauce, salt, and cayenne and cook for 7 to 10 minutes over low heat, stirring frequently.

Spoon the potatoes onto plates and serve with plenty of ketchup on the side.

Chapter 7

---◇---

Tempting Desserts and Happy Endings

Traditionally, American desserts are prepared with a lot of butter, milk, cream, and eggs. When it comes to calories, the sky is the limit. Vegan desserts, on the other hand, feature a cornucopia of seasonal and dried fruits, wholesome grains, and light spices. Recipes with apples, bananas, peaches, summer berries, mangoes, and kiwifruits fill the vegan dessert menu. Additionally, dairy-free alternatives, such as soy milk, rice milk, and silken tofu, inspire a medley of refreshing fruit shakes.

This chapter offers an array of fruity desserts and creative treats, from Mango-Banana Flambé and Apple-Pineapple Crisp to Piña Colada Rice Pudding and Tofu Kiwi-Berry Shake. All of these vegan desserts are healthful, easy to prepare, and a pleasure to devour. Here is delicious proof that it is possible to enjoy a taste of something sweet without resorting to the usual lineup of eggs, butter, and dairy products.

With a little creativity and imagination, these tempting recipes can enliven and enrich the vegan lifestyle.

Mango-Banana Flambé

*For this grand finale, tropical mango and bananas are
simmered in a sweet sauce of apple juice, rum, cinnamon,
and brown sugar.*

Yield: 4 servings

¼	cup apple juice
2	to 3 tablespoons brown sugar
1	large ripe mango, peeled, pitted, and sliced
3	or 4 bananas, peeled and sliced crosswise
¼	teaspoon ground cinnamon or nutmeg
¼	cup dark rum
	Splash of banana liqueur (optional)

In a large skillet, combine the apple juice and brown sugar.
Cook over medium heat for about 3 minutes, stirring
frequently. Add the mango, bananas, and cinnamon and cook
for 3 to 4 minutes, stirring occasionally. Turn the slices gently,
coating them with the juice mixture.

Remove the pan from the heat and add the rum and optional liqueur. Return to the heat and bring to a simmer over medium heat. Carefully touch a lighted match to the pan, "flaming" the fruit. Allow the flame to subside and continue cooking for 1 minute.

Spoon the fruit onto warm plates and serve at once. A frozen nondairy dessert (such as frozen rice milk) makes a fine companion.

Helpful Tip:

When flambéing (or flaming) the fruit, never pour liquor directly from the bottle to the pan. Always measure out the liquor and transfer it to a small pitcher ahead of time.

Cinnamon Applesauce

The aroma of apples simmering on the stove top is a sure sign that autumn has arrived. This simple, homemade applesauce is a delightful treat anytime of day or night.

Yield: 4 cups

8	tart apples, cored and diced (do not peel)
4	to 5 tablespoons water
2	tablespoons vegan honey
½	teaspoon ground cinnamon

In a medium saucepan, combine the apples and water. Cook over medium heat for 25 to 30 minutes, stirring occasionally, until the apples have a mashed consistency. Stir in the honey and cinnamon. Remove the apples from the heat and let cool for about 5 minutes.

Transfer the mashed apples to a blender and blend until smooth, about 5 seconds (for a chunky sauce, mash the apples with a spoon by hand). Chill the sauce for at least 1 hour before serving.

Pumpkin-Raisin Scones

Scones, sometimes referred to as tea biscuits, make excellent companions to a cup of hot tea or coffee. This version's mild pumpkin flavor is accented with cinnamon and nutmeg.

Yield: 20 to 24 small scones

2½	cups all-purpose unbleached flour
2½	teaspoons baking powder
1	teaspoon ground cinnamon
½	teaspoon ground nutmeg
½	teaspoon salt
¼	cup brown sugar
¼	cup vegan margarine, softened
1	can (16 ounces) pumpkin puree
1	cup soy milk or rice milk
⅓	cup dark raisins

Preheat the oven to 400 degrees F. Lightly grease 2 baking pans.

In a medium mixing bowl, combine the flour, baking powder, cinnamon, nutmeg, salt, and sugar. Cut in the margarine until the dough resembles coarse meal. With a large mixing spoon, blend in the pumpkin and milk; mix until fully incorporated. Fold in the raisins.

Drop or scoop 2 to 3 tablespoons of batter at a time onto the baking sheets, forming round balls. Scoop all of the batter onto the pans. Place in the oven and bake until the crust of the scones are lightly browned, 12 to 14 minutes. Let the scones cool to room temperature.

Serve with a hot beverage.

Apple-Pineapple Crisp

Pineapple lends a tropical twist to this crunchy apple crisp delight.

Yield: 6 servings

1	can (20 ounces) pineapple rings, drained
2	large tart apples, sliced
2	tablespoons vegan honey
	Juice of 1 lime
½	teaspoon ground nutmeg
½	cup old-fashioned "rolled" oatmeal
½	cup unbleached all-purpose flour
½	cup brown sugar
½	teaspoon ground cinnamon
4	tablespoons vegan margarine

Preheat the oven to 375 degrees F.

In a mixing bowl, combine the pineapple, apples, honey, lime juice, and nutmeg. Spread the fruit mixture over the bottom of an 8-inch-square baking dish.

In a large mixing bowl, combine the oatmeal, flour, sugar, and cinnamon. With a fork or pastry tool, cut the margarine into the dry ingredients until the mixture has a crumbled texture. Sprinkle the topping evenly over the fruit. Place the pan in the oven and bake until the fruit is tender and the topping is lightly browned, 25 to 30 minutes.

Remove from the oven and serve warm. If desired, offer a frozen nondairy dessert (such as frozen rice milk) on the side.

Fruity Rice Pudding

Most traditional rice puddings are turbo-caloried desserts loaded with heavy cream, sugar, and even eggs. This nondairy alternative features rice milk (or soy milk), apples, and dried fruits.

Yield: 4 servings

2½	cups cooked short-grain brown or white rice
1½	cups rice milk or soy milk
1	medium red apple, diced
⅓	cup brown sugar
½	cup dried apricots, chopped
¼	cup dark raisins
½	teaspoon ground cinnamon
½	teaspoon ground nutmeg

In a medium saucepan, combine the cooked rice, milk, apple, sugar, apricots, raisins, and cinnamon. Cook over medium-low heat, stirring frequently, until the rice is thick and the fruit is tender, about 15 minutes. Remove from the heat and let cool slightly. Transfer the pudding to a bowl and refrigerate for at least 1 hour before serving.

When ready to serve, spoon the rice pudding into bowls and sprinkle some of the nutmeg over the top of each bowl.

Mexican-Style Rice Pudding

Mexican rice puddings are often cooked with whole cinnamon sticks and the peel of a citrus fruit. The combination of flavors yields a flavorful pudding with a fragrant nuance.

Yield: 6 servings

2½	cups rice milk
2	cups cooked white or brown rice
½	cup white sugar
¼	cup dark raisins
3	to 4 tablespoons grated sweetened coconut
½	teaspoon vanilla extract
1	whole cinnamon stick
1	(2-inch) strip of lime or orange peel

In a medium saucepan, combine the milk, rice, sugar, raisins, coconut, vanilla, cinnamon stick, and lime peel. Cook over medium-low heat, stirring frequently, until the rice is thick and the fruit is tender, about 30 minutes. Remove from the heat and let cool slightly. Transfer the pudding to a bowl and refrigerate for at least 1 hour before serving.

When ready to serve, remove the cinnamon stick and citrus peel and discard. Spoon the rice pudding into bowls and serve at once. If desired, garnish each bowl with a twist of lime or orange peel.

Piña Colada
Rice Pudding

The scrumptious trio of pineapple, coconut, and rum gives this Caribbean-inspired rice pudding a tropical personality.

Yield: 6 servings

3	cups cooked white or brown rice
1	cup canned coconut milk
1	can (15 ounces) diced pineapple, with liquid
½	cup brown or white sugar
¼	cup dark raisins
3	tablespoons dark rum
½	teaspoon ground nutmeg

In a medium saucepan, combine the rice, coconut milk, pineapple and liquid, sugar, raisins, and rum. Cook for 10 to 12 minutes over medium-low heat, stirring frequently. Remove from the heat and let cool slightly. Chill for at least 1 hour before serving.

When ready to serve, spoon the pudding into bowls and sprinkle some of the nutmeg over each bowl. If desired, garnish each with a swizzle stick.

Strawberry-Orange Sorbet

A palate-cleansing frozen sorbet makes a perfect treat when you're craving something light—but still a little sweet.

Yield: 8 servings

1	cup apple juice
1	cup orange juice
½	cup white sugar
2	pints fresh strawberries, diced (about 4 cups)
2	tablespoons Triple Sec or other orange liqueur
	Juice of 1 lime

In a medium saucepan, combine the apple juice, orange juice, and sugar and bring to a simmer over medium heat. Cook for about 10 minutes, stirring occasionally. Stir in the strawberries, Triple Sec, and lime juice, remove from the heat, and set aside for 5 minutes.

Add the strawberry mixture to a food processor fitted with a steel blade or to a blender and process until liquefied, about 10 seconds. Transfer the mixture to a plastic container with a lid and freeze for 2 to 4 hours or overnight (stir the sorbet one or two times after about 1 hour).

To serve, scoop the sorbet into small serving bowls and serve at once.

Holiday Mango "Egg" Nog

While traditional eggnogs are made with heavy cream and eggs (and ooze with fat and calories), this light, dairy-free version is enriched with mangos, bananas, and vanilla-flavored rice milk.

Yield: 3 to 4 servings

1	ripe mango, peeled, pitted, and chopped
1	or 2 bananas, peeled and chopped
2	cups vanilla rice milk or vanilla soy milk
2	to 3 tablespoons dark rum
1	tablespoon vegan honey
1	teaspoon vanilla extract
½	teaspoon ground nutmeg

Combine the mango, banana, milk, rum, honey, vanilla, and nutmeg in a blender and blend until creamy, 10 to 15 seconds.

Pour the nog into glasses and serve at once.

Tofu Kiwi-Berry Shake

This creamy fruit shake is made with silken tofu, a soft, almost liquid version of soybean curd. This treat makes a healthful beverage anytime of the day.

Yield: 2 servings

2	cups silken tofu
2	cups fresh or frozen strawberries or blueberries (thawed, if frozen)
2	medium kiwifruits, peeled and diced
2	bananas, diced
¼	teaspoon ground nutmeg

Combine the tofu, berries, kiwi, bananas, and nutmeg in a blender and process until creamy, 5 to 10 seconds.

Pour the shake into cold glasses and serve as a beverage or dessert.

Blueberry-Banana Smoothie

Here is an easy recipe with which to experiment with alternative milk products, such as oat milk, almond milk, or flavored rice milk. It's as creamy as a milk shake and a snap to make.

Yield: 2 large servings

2	cups almond milk or oat milk
1½	cups fresh or frozen blueberries (thawed, if frozen)
2	bananas, diced
2	tablespoons wheat germ (optional)

Combine the milk, blueberries, bananas, and optional wheat germ in a blender and process until smooth, about 5 seconds.

Pour the smoothies into tall glasses and serve as a beverage or light dessert.

Poached Fruit in Red Wine

Poaching peaches and nectarines in red wine is an elegant way to enjoy the delicious fruits of summer.

Yield: 8 servings

1	bottle dry red wine
⅓	cup vegan honey
¼	teaspoon ground nutmeg
2	or 3 black peppercorns
1	(1-inch) strip lemon or lime zest
4	large peaches, halved and pitted
4	large nectarines, halved and pitted
20	to 24 ounces frozen rice milk

In a large saucepan, combine the wine, honey, nutmeg, pepper-corns, and lemon zest and bring to a simmer over medium heat. Add the fruit to the pan and return to a simmer. Reduce the heat to low and cook for 8 to 12 minutes, until the fruit is tender. Using a slotted spoon remove the fruit and place in a shallow bowl. Let the fruit cool for a few minutes and then cover and refrigerate for 2 hours or overnight.

Continue to simmer the poaching liquid over medium-high heat for about 10 minutes more, stirring frequently, until the sauce is syrupy and reduced by about half. Remove from the heat and let cool for a few minutes. Cover and refrigerate for 2 hours or overnight.

When ready to serve, using a slotted spoon, arrange the fruit on small serving plates. Drizzle the wine sauce over the fruit and serve the frozen rice milk on the side.

Hawaiian Coconut Pudding

This tropical dessert, known as "haupia," has a luscious texture and rich nutty coconut flavor. A little spoon of it goes a long way.

Yield: 6 to 8 servings

¼	cup sugar
¼	cup cornstarch
1½	cups canned coconut milk
1	tablespoon vanilla extract

In a small bowl combine the sugar and cornstarch and set aside.

In a small, sturdy saucepan combine the coconut milk and vanilla extract and bring to a gentle simmer over medium heat, stirring frequently. Reduce the heat to low and cook, stirring, for 4 to 5 minutes. Whisk the sugar mixture into the coconut milk and cook, stirring, until the mixture thickens (like pudding), about 3 to 4 minutes. Remove the pan from the heat.

Pour the pudding into an 8-inch square pan, lightly cover, and refrigerate until firm, about 2 to 3 hours. Cut the pudding into small squares and serve.

Index

warm Thai, soy vinaigrette
with, 130

O

Onions
bulgur pilaf with, 156
caramelized, mizuna salad
with, 49
sautéed, lentil and kale stew with,
34–35
yellow spice rice with, 153
Orange-strawberry sorbet, 224
Orzo and sweet pea pilaf, 150–151
Oven-roasted sweet plantains, 206

P

Papayas
guacamole, 102–103
-mango vinaigrette, 81
Parboiled rice, about, 141
Parsley soup, *caldo verde,* 10–11
Parsnips, about, 195
Pasta, *see also* Noodles
about, 107–108
and bean soup, 38–39
bow-tie, with balsamic herb
vinaigrette, 72
country ragu with, 124
Creole ragu with, 118–119
garden tomato sauce with,
120–121
macaroni
eggplant ratatouille with,
114–115
hot chili, 109
marinara with broccoli, 110–111
oven-broiled vegetables
with, 117
penne
and artichoke salad, 70–71
Swiss chard with, 116
rigatoni, ratatouille red sauce with,
136–137
salad, Santa Fe, 48
spaghetti
arrabiata with, 125
garden greens with, 112
mushroom marinara with, 113
ziti, exotic mushrooms with,
134–135

Pasta e fagiole, 38–39
Peanuts
dressing, with Asian noodles,
46–47
-lime sauce, Javanese noodles
with, 126–127
sauce, spicy, somen noodles
with, 53
stew, West African, 212–213
tofu and rice salad, Javanese, 60
Peas, *see specific peas*
Penne
and artichoke salad, 70–71
Swiss chard with, 116
Peppers, *see specific peppers*
Pilafs
artichoke, lemony, 152
asparagus, artichokes with, 148
barley, powerhouse, 166
bulgur, vegetables with, 156
multigrain vegetable, 149
noodles, Middle Eastern, 132–133
orzo and sweet pea, 150–151
quinoa, stove-top, 162–163
squash, savory, 181
sweet potato, 182–183
Piña colada rice pudding, 223
Pineapples
-apple crisps, 220
-mango chutney, 92
Piquant creole sauce, 99
Pita bread salad, 55
Plantains, oven-roasted sweet, 206
Poached fruit in red wine, 228
Poblano peppers
hummus dip with, 82–83
rice with, Mexican, 161
Porotos granados, 200
Potatoes
about, 191–192
artichoke and white bean stew, 211
and beet salad, gourmet, 68–69
curried
chick-peas with, 179
lentils with, Indian, 176–177
spinach with, 207
gnocchi, eggplant stew with,
128–129
and green pea soup, curried,
26–27
hash browns, spinach, 214

International Conversion Chart

These are not exact equivalents: they have been slightly rounded to make measuring easier.

LIQUID MEASUREMENTS

American	Imperial	Metric	Australian
2 tablespoons (1 oz.)	1 fl. oz.	30 ml	1 tablespoon
1/4 cup (2 oz.)	2 fl. oz.	60 ml	2 tablespoons
1/3 cup (3 oz.)	3 fl. oz.	80 ml	1/4 cup
1/2 cup (4 oz.)	4 fl. oz.	125 ml	1/3 cup
2/3 cup (5 oz.)	5 fl. oz.	165 ml	1/2 cup
3/4 cup (6 oz.)	6 fl. oz.	185 ml	2/3 cup
1 cup (8 oz.)	8 fl. oz.	250 ml	3/4 cup

SPOON MEASUREMENTS

American	Metric
1/4 teaspoon	1 ml
1/2 teaspoon	2 ml
1 teaspoon	5 ml
1 tablespoon	15 ml

WEIGHTS

US/UK	Metric
1 oz.	30 grams (g)
2 oz.	60 g
4 oz. (1/4 lb)	125 g
5 oz. (1/3 lb)	155 g
6 oz.	185 g
7 oz.	220 g
8 oz. (1/2 lb)	250 g
10 oz.	315 g
12 oz. (3/4 lb)	375 g
14 oz.	440 g
16 oz. (1 lb)	500 g
2 lbs	1 kg

OVEN TEMPERATURES

Farenheit	Centigrade	Gas
250	120	1/2
300	150	2
325	160	3
350	180	4
375	190	5
400	200	6
450	230	8

Sumptuous Recipes for the Miracle Food of the '90s!

Soy, in all of its forms, has long been an international staple in vegetarian cooking. In this groundbreaking book, Dana Jacobi proves just how versatile—and flavorful—soy can be. Her collection of innovative recipes brings a variety of soy products to life in mouthwatering and satisfying combinations. Among the delicious recipes are Fresh Coriander Soup, Savory Black Olive and Rosemary Biscotti, Smokin' Black Soybean Chili with Corn, and the Creamiest Tofu Cheesecake in the World.

PRIMA

To Order Books

Please send me the following items:

Quantity	Title	Unit Price	Total
_____	**101 Meatless Family Dishes**	**$ 14.95**	$ _____
_____	**Lean and Luscious and Meatless**	**$ 19.95**	$ _____
_____	**The Complete Book of Juicing**	**$ 14.00**	$ _____
_____	**The Natural Kitchen: Soy!**	**$ 14.00**	$ _____
_____	_____	$ _____	$ _____

	Subtotal $ _____
	7.25% Sales Tax (CA only) $ _____
	7% Sales Tax (PA only) $ _____
	5% Sales Tax (IN only) $ _____
	7% G.S.T. Tax (Canada only) $ _____
	Shipping and Handling $ _____
	Total Order $ _____

FREE
Ground Freight
in U.S. and Canada

Foreign and all Priority Request orders:
Call Customer Service
for price quote at 916-632-4400

By Telephone: With American Express, MC, or Visa,
call 800-632-8676 or 916-632-4400. Mon–Fri, 8:30–4:30.
WWW: http://www.primapublishing.com

By Internet E-mail: sales@primapub.com
By Mail: Just fill out the information below and send with your remittance to:

Prima Publishing
P.O. Box 1260BK
Rocklin, CA 95677

Name _____

Address _____

City _____ State _____ ZIP_____

American Express/MC/Visa# _____ Exp. _____

Check/money order enclosed for $_____ Payable to Prima Publishing

Daytime telephone _____

Signature _____